# On Private Indirect Government

# State of the Literature Series

**Les théories du post-ajustment: quelques pistes de recherche pour les économies africaines** (1-1998)

Hakim Ben Hammouda

**Du gouvernement privé indirecte** (1-1999)

Achille Mbembe

**Science politique réflexive et savoirs sur les pratiques politiques en Afrique noire** (2-1999)

Luc Sindjoun

**Post-Adjustment theories: a few research trails for African economies** (2-2000)

Hakim Ben Hammouda

# On Private Indirect Government

Achille Mbembe

State of the Literature Series

No. 1 - 2000

On Private Indirect Government

State of the Literature Series 1/2000

© Council for the Development of Social Science Research in Africa 2000

Translated from the French **Du gouvernement privé indirect**

© Council for the Development of Social Science Research in Africa 1999

Avenue Cheikh Anta Diop, BP 3304, Dakar, Senegal

**ISSN 0851-0466**

Typesetting by Djibril Fall

Printed by CODESRIA

CODESRIA would like to express its gratitude to the Swedish Agency for International Development Cooperation Agency (SIDA/SAREC), the International Development Research Centre (IDRC), the Ford Foundation, the MacArthur Foundation, the Carnegie Corporation, the Norwegian Ministry of Foreign Affairs, the Danish Agency for International Development (DANIDA) the French Ministry of Cooperation, the United Nations Development Programme, the Netherlands Ministry of Foreign Affairs, the Rockefeller Foundation, and the Government of Senegal for their support of its research, training and publications programmes.

# Contents

## Part One

## The Right to Use

## Part Two

## The Price of Force

# The Author

Achille Mbembe is currently Executive Secretary of the Council for the Development of Social Science Research in Africa (CODESRIA). He was professor of history at Columbia University, New York and the University of Pennsylavania, Philadelphia, United States. He is the author of numerous publications, among these include *La naissance d'un maquis dans le sud Cameroun (1920-60): histoire des usages de la raison en colonie* (Paris Karthala, 1996); *Les Jeunes et l'Ordre Politique en Afrique Noire* (Paris: L'Harmattan, 1985); *La Politique par le Bas en Afrique Noire: Contributions à une Problématique de la Démocratie* (Paris: Editions Karthala, 1992) co-authored with Jean-François Bayart and Comi Toulabor ; and *Afriques Indociles: Christianisme, Pouvoir et Etat en Société Post Coloniale* (Paris: Editions Karthala, 1988).

## Introduction

The aim of this study is to draw attention to the long time-scale of the developments currently taking place in Africa. This has been overshadowed by the brouhaha concerning phenomena that are mainly connected with the present moment (structural adjustment, transitions toward democracy, wars and conflicts, corruption, criminalization).

This study is based on two hypotheses. The first is that of interlacing: emerging from a history whose depth is overlooked by many analysts, Africa is simultaneously advancing in several directions. This advance is not following a closed orbit. It is neither smooth nor unilinear. It is heading toward several outcomes at once. Moreover, it is moving on several time-scales and takes the form of fluctuations and destabilizations, sometimes abrupt, as well as of apparently disordered accelerations and inertias. In fact, however, several different systems of change are involved: stationary, dynamic, volatile, even catastrophic.

The second hypothesis is that of the exit of the state. This exit is neither total nor irreversible. It takes diverse forms. Some of them will be examined later in this study. For the moment, it facilitates the emergence of new political actors in the public sphere, the proliferation of unexpected social rationalities, and the implementation of novel technologies and apparatuses, whose purpose is to control individual conduct and to make possible new modes of constituting private property and inequality.

Private indirect government: this is the formula we propose to apply to these emergent technologies of domination, whose forms, intrinsic qualities, and goals are fundamentally different from those which postcolonial African regimes had previously espoused. Private indirect government is itself the result of an abrupt renegotiation of the relationships between the privatization of public violence, on the one hand, and the constitution of

1

new systems of private property on the other. Our attention will be focused here on this privatization of public violence, this appropriation of substances and profits, the levies they require, the shifting of boundaries to which they lead, and the new forms of violence and social stratification to which they imply.

# Part One

# The Right to Use

The aim of the first part of this study is twofold. First, at a rather general level, we shall reflect on the types of rationality that have been put into operation, since the end of direct colonization, to control individuals and human collectivities and to ensure an increasing number of goods and objects in sub-Saharan Africa. Secondly, we shall examine the conditions in which the activity that consists in "controlling people's conduct within the framework of a state and with the state's instruments" (that is, the activity of governing) has recently passed out of the hands of those who were supposed to exercise it, thus opening the way, not to a revolution of some kind, but to an extraordinary situation of material scarcity, uncertainty, and inertia.

So far as the activity of governing is concerned, two things come to mind. First, dealing with human conduct and the ways in which it is governed within the framework of a state and with its instruments involves not only discovering what constitutes the power and reason of the state, but also taking an interest in power's forms and manifestations, the techniques it uses to increase its value, to distribute the products of labor, to ensure abundance or to manage want and scarcity. And since in Africa, both before and after colonization, state power increased its value by implementing specific relationships of subjection, we will be led to discuss the connections among relationships of subjection (what was called "command"), the distribution of wealth and benefits, and the more general problem of the constitution of the postcolonial subject. On the other hand, African postcolonial regimes did not invent their knowledge of government *ex nihilo*. This knowledge was drawn from several cultures, heritages, and traditions, whose elements interlaced through time, resulting in the weaving of a fabric which gestures toward "custom" without being reducible to it, and participates in "modernity" without being entirely identical with it. One of these kinds of knowledge or rationalities is colonial rationality, which we shall now proceed to describe briefly.

5

## On Command

In a colony, "command" was based upon an outlook or *imaginaire* very specific to state sovereignty. State sovereignty had two main characteristics. One the one hand, there was both a weakness and an inflation of the law. A weakness of the law, to the extent that in the relations between power and authority, the colonial model was, in theory as in practice, the exact opposite of the liberal model of discussion or deliberation. An inflation of the law, in the sense that except when it was exercised in the form of arbitrariness and the right of conquest, the very concept of law was often revealed to be void of content. On the other hand, colonial sovereignty was based on three kinds of violence.[1]

The first of these was a foundational violence that posited and authorized not only the right of conquest, but all the other prerogatives the latter entailed. In this respect, it had an instituting function, for at least two reasons. On the one hand, it helped create the very object of its violence. One can say that in this way, it presupposed itself. On the other hand, it considered itself the sole competent judge of its laws. Hence its unilateral nature, all the more so because—to adopt Hegel's formula—through its ability to take upon itself the act of destruction, its supreme law was at the same time the supreme negation of law.

A second form of violence was produced both before and after the fact, or even in the wake of conquest itself. It was a kind of legitimation. As Derrida points out in a different context, its function was to provide the colonial order with a language and self-interpreting models, to give it a meaning, to justify its necessity and its universalizing mission—in short, to

---

[1] Here, I take my inspiration from remarks made by Jacques Derrida in another context. See his *Force de loi* (Paris: Galilée, 1994): 81-83.

help it produce an imagination whose effect was to convert the foundational violence into an authorizing authority.

The third form was supposed to ensure maintenance, increase, and permanence. Clearly distinguishing itself from war in the strict sense of the word, it constantly replicated itself, in the most banal and ordinary situations. It was later crystallized in a collection of countless acts and rites; in sum, it played such an important role in everyday life that it ended up constituting something like the central *imaginaire* of a culture that the state shared with society.[2] Its function was thus to ratify and reiterate.

Colonial sovereignty existed only when these three forms of violence were in position. In that case, they formed a single, self-identical web. Immediately tangible, this singular violence gave natives a perspective of themselves in proportion to the power of which it had deprived them. Its peculiarity was to express itself in both forms of authority and forms of morality. Authority and morality for two reasons. First because in it every distinction between means and ends was abolished. Depending on the circumstances that obtained, this sovereign violence was its own end and its own mode of application. Secondly, because the result was an almost unlimited permutation of the just and the unjust, of the lawful and the unlawful. So far as colonial sovereignty was concerned, right and law were on one side alone. They were embodied in the very occurrence of the act. Confronted by it, there could be only "wrong-doing" and infraction. Anyone who did not recognize this violence's authority and challenged its protocols was considered a savage and an outlaw.

---

[2]   See for example the image of "Bula Matari." Cf. B. Jewsiewicki and C. Young, "Painting the Burden of the Past: History as Tragedy," in B. Jewsiewicki, ed., *Art pictural zaïrois* (Quebec: Éditions du Septentrion, 1992), 117-138.

The power of this conflation, combined with the power of disqualification, resulted in "command" asking itself few questions about its goals, since it was the very authority that justified them. That is why, in implementing its projects, the colonial state did not hesitate to resort to brute force in dealing with natives, to destroy the forms of social organization that previously existed, or even to co-opt these forms in the service of ends other than those to which they had earlier been directed. The injustice of the means and the illegitimacy of the goals combined to make room for a certain arbitrariness, a certain intrinsic unconditionality, that might be said to be the peculiar characteristic of colonial sovereignty. Postcolonial governmental forms have inherited this unconditionality and the system of impunity that was its corollary.

How can this unconditionality and impunity be explained, if not by reference to what long constituted the credo of power in the colonies? In this respect, two traditions have to be distinguished. Both accord a central role to a representation of the colonized individual, which made of him the very prototype of the animal.[3] On the one hand, there was what we call the Hegelian tradition, according to which the colonized individual who was subordinate to power and the state could not be like "myself." As an animal, he is strictly alien to me. His way of viewing the world, that is, his mode of being, is not mine. No power of transcending himself can be perceived in him. Encapsulated in himself, he is a bundle of drives, not abilities.

---

[3]  The idea of exploring this aspect of the question was suggested by Wambui Mwangi. To organize the following reflections, I have drawn heavily on the studies on "the animal" contained in the journal *Alter* 3 (1995) and in the special number of *Social Research* 62 (1995) on the theme "In the Company of Animals."

Given these conditions, the only possible relationship to him is one of violence, servitude, and domination. Within this relationship, the colonized individual can be envisaged only as power's property, something that belongs to it. He is a tool subordinated to those who, having made him, can employ him and modify him as they wish. In this respect, he belongs to the sphere of objects. They can be destroyed, just as one can kill an animal, cut it up, cook it, and, if need be, eat it. To that extent, in the colony the body of the colonized individual is considered, in its profanity, one object among others. Indeed, being no more than a "body-thing," it is neither the substrate nor the affirmation of any mind or spirit. As for the colonized individual's death, it matters little whether it happens as a suicide, a homicide, or is inflicted upon him by power: strictly speaking, it has absolutely no connection with any kind of work that power is supposed to be doing for the common good. His cadaver remains lying on the earth in a sort of unshakable rigidity, a material mass and a simple, inert object, condemned in the position of that which plays no role at all.

In addition, there was a tradition that could be called Bergsonian. It was based on the notion that one can sympathize with the colonized individual, even "love" him, just as one might an animal. Thus it is sad when he dies, because up to a point he is part of the familiar world. Affection for the colonized individual can also be expressed by gestures. In return, the colonized individual has to give his master the same affection that the latter gives him. But beyond gestures, the master's affection for the animal is especially felt as an interior force that is supposed to govern the animal. In the Bergsonian tradition of colonialism, the relationship of familiarity and domestication is substituted for the relationship of servitude. Through the relationship of domestication, the master leads the animal to have an experience such that ultimately the animal, while remaining what it is— different from man—nonetheless really comes into the world for his master.

The colonized individual can enter the world for his master only after a process of training. The colonist can inculcate habits in the colonized individual, treat him violently if necessary, speak to him as if to a child, reprimand him, congratulate him. But above all, the colonized individual, just like the animal, is an object of experimentation in a game the colonist plays with himself, even while recognizing that between himself and the colonized individual, there is no community of essence. Heidegger reminds us that "we do not live with them if living means: being like an animal. Nonetheless, we are with them. This being together is, however, not a matter of existing together, to the extent that a dog does not exist but only lives. This being together with animals is such that we allow these animals to move within our world." Thus to command an animal (the slave or the colonized person) is to play a game that consists in trying to get it to move beyond its limits, while at the same time knowing full well that these limits will never be overcome, because the animal's impulses are almost always determined by training and domestication. In other words, it amounts to playing this game while at the same time being aware of the fact even if the animal (the colonized individual) is part of the familiar world, even if he has needs (for food, water, copulation, etc.), he can never really enter the sphere of human possibility. Because of the kind of life peculiar to him, he belongs to the sphere of life-forms that are defined by their confinement within the bounds of virtuality and contingency.

Under colonization, the object and the subject[4] of command consisted of a specific category: the 'indigene'. In the strict sense of the word, the 'indigene' is a person who was born in the country in question. In this respect, it resembles the term "native," which designates a person whose roots are in the same

---

[4]   I use the notion of "subject" to designate a person who is *subjected* to sovereign domination.

area in which he lives, and who has not immigrated there. But in the political vocabulary of colonialism, the term "indigene" refers to the colonized subject in general. Not only were indigenes as a whole seen as the "formless clay of the primitive multitudes" (Albert Sarraut) on which colonization was supposed to shape "the face of a new humanity," but also the *indigénat* itself was a special kind of administrative system applied to the autochthonous peoples in a colony, as opposed to the colonists.[5] This system was a caricatural way of putting the mark of colonial sovereignty on the structures of colonized peoples' everyday life. As a penal system, it included a whole range of punishments covering countless offenses. These punishments were administered by a central state apparatus, or more precisely, by its agents, through a series of specialized institutions. Some of these institutions were of recent origin, while others were autochthonous, but reconfigured to suit current needs.

Whatever the forms and nature of the rituals of punishment, they all bore upon the body of the colonized individual. As a force of production, he was in fact set apart, trained, compelled to do heavy work, obliged to observe formalities—the objective being not only to make him docile and to bring him into submission, but also to extract from him the maximum possible usefulness. The colonial relationship qua relationship of subjection was, in fact, inseparable from specific modalities of punishment and from a concern for productivity at the same time. In the latter regard, it differs qualitatively from the postcolonial relationship.

One of the characteristics of command in the colonies, however, was precisely the conflation of the public and private spheres. The colony's agents could at any time take possession of the law and the colony's surpluses in order to use

---

5    See R. Buell, *The Native Problem in Africa* (New York: Macmillan, 1928), and also A. Ashforth, *The Politics of Official Discourse in South Africa* (Oxford: Clarendon Press, 1990).

them for purely private advantage. However, violence in the colonies was characterized by miniaturization. It was exercised, so to speak, in detail. It tended to emerge at any time, on any pretext, and anywhere. It was deployed in a segmented manner, in the form of micro-arrangements that constantly miniaturized themselves and thereby produced a multitude of small fears.

As for the colonists, it should be emphasized that for a long time (in the ancien régime's colonial system as restored by Napoleon, for instance), they alone enjoyed what substituted for civil and political freedoms.[6] Thus in Martinique, Guadeloupe, and French Guyana, the principles of equality before the law, freedoms, and rights to property, which issued from the French Revolution of 1789, were thwarted by the persistence of an economic system that depended on slavery. Planters exercised their domination over slaves by means of racial discrimination, punishment, torture, and cruelty, and they saw the legal system as the guarantee that the laws and brute force ought to provide for their properties. Until 1828, the penal code and the codes of both civil and criminal prosecution recognized only two categories of individuals: freemen and slaves.[7]

This distinction was based on race. Freemen, that is, essentially, white people, had rights to the slaves' (that is, colored people's) labor, and could raise money by using them as security. They could rent them to their peers, who put them to work. This was often the case among small slave-owners, who charged a set fee per head for a year's labor, occasionally sold their slaves, and expropriated any property slaves had amassed or saved, thus sanctioning a

---

[6]  Cf. J. Saintoyant, *La colonisation française pendant la période napoléonienne (1799-1815)* (Paris: La Renaissance du Livre, 1931); this work seeks to justify French colonial policies.

[7]  The first steps toward civil equality were taken under  Charles X.  Some fundamental transformations took place after the revolution of 1830.  For

general system of despoliation that remained in place until 1848. In order to divide up reality, make use of men and objects, and create useful goods, command thus proceeded by attribution and designation. The value attached to human beings and their rights depended on this classification. The same held true for the deprivations to which they might be subjected, the suffering and degradation that might be inflicted upon them, and even the satisfactions to which they could aspire.

In order to understand the particularity of this mode of power's existence within the framework of the colony, we have to emphasize four of its chief characteristics, which are also to be found in various forms in most postcolonial African societies. First, the colonial mode of exercising power was part of an exceptional system, that is, one whose peculiar feature was that it violated what was supposed to be common law. This violation of common law was accompanied by the delegation of kingly rights to private individuals and the constitution, by these private individuals, of a form of sovereignty that drew some of its attributes from royal power itself.[8] For example, the ties between the king (who granted the franchise) and the company (the franchise holder) resembled in some respects the ties between a feudal lord and his vassal.

The attribution of almost royal prerogatives and rights to companies of ordinary merchants and the latter's enjoyment of almost sovereign privileges in fact belonged to a tradition that went back to the Middle Ages. We know that

---

example, a law passed on 24 February 1831 granted full civil rights to so-called people of color. Two years later, in 1833, people of color acquired, in theory, the right to vote and to be elected. In practice, the bar that had been provided by racial discrimination was converted into another one: a high property or income qualification.

[8] See E. Petit, *Droit public ou gouvernement des colonies françaises d'après les lois faites pour ces pays* (Paris: Librairie Paul Geuthner, 1771).

from the Middle Ages to the Renaissance, a steadily increasing number of lords acquired the right to dispense justice at all levels, both low and high. Many were able to levy troops and taxes, and carry on their own wars. The social and political order, composed of powerful closed corporations, religious orders, and influential military men, was itself based on the existence of differential rights, privileges, and monopolies, whether these had to do with commerce, trade, honors, or titles. Throughout the colonial period, there was a connection between these arrangements and the culture of power that developed in the conquered lands.

Secondly, the colonial way of regulating people's conduct and creating useful goods within a state framework and with the tools of the state was from the outset part of a system of favors and immunities. In fact, the ancien régime had not only made franchised companies the privileged vehicle of colonization, but had also granted them exorbitant powers that were then called "favors." The latter consisted mainly in the right to establish and to collect certain taxes, to receive income, to mint money, to arm and maintain at their own cost troops for the defense of their agents or for conquest, to wage war, to make peace, to sign treaties, and to grant titles and honors.[9] These favors were accompanied by a range of privileges. For example, merchandise transported by the company could be exempted from certain customs duties or transit taxes. The companies alone had the power to bring colonists into the territory. Sometimes having full ownership of the land, they could, completely or at least to a certain extent, do what they wanted with it; they alone could sell or grant lands in exchange for rents or royalties. Finally, they alone enjoyed the privilege of being able conduct commerce between France and the company's territory.[10]

---

[9]   L. Cordier, *Les compagnies à charte et la politique coloniale sous le ministère de Colbert* (Geneva: Slatkine-Megariotis Reprints, 1976), 72-76.

[10]   J. Chailley-Bert, *Les compagnies de colonisation sous l'ancien régime* (New York: Burt Franklin, 1898).

At the foundation of this way of exercising power, then, there was a group of privileges that were granted to individuals, outside the common law. In contrast to the prerogative that consisted in a portion of the royal domain being granted to younger sons in compensation for excluding them from the throne, privilege, both in the ancien régime and later on, had the particularity of being an advantage that was always enjoyed to the disadvantage of others. Favors were the result of the king's good will, and might be converted into advantages and profits. They also served to build up power. Thus, for example, laws and regulations were tailored to the needs of the colonists. Laws might be modified either through rulings or through special arrangements made by the colonial authorities, to whom the king granted the right to make laws. Judgment could be summary and without appeal. It was not supposed to be expensive. The right of preemption, the protection of the company's privileges, expropriation and confiscation, to its own profit, of merchandise sold and transported in violation of its privilege, recourse to armed force—all this was common.

Subsequently, the powers whose exercise affected the population's honor, life, work, and property were conferred on bureaucrats. Almost everywhere, except in the three colonies of Martinique, Réunion, and Guadeloupe, the primordial rights (political rights, representation, civil status, property, contracts and obligations) were subject to arbitrary decree. Religion, the press, lending institutions, administrative powers, public works, police, and criminal penalties were governed, in law, by decisions made by the government in Paris, that is, by the changing views of a minister or secretary of state, of a department head or an agent appointed through favor.[11] The

---

[11] The representation of the colonies in the Parlement was recognized *de jure* and *de facto* by the French Revolution. But it was abolished in 1800. Rejected by the Restoration and the July monarchy, it was once again granted by the

ideal of freedom and autonomy was thwarted by the impunity enjoyed by the proconsuls and by the omnipotence of the agents of power.

The third characteristic of the colonial mode of exercising power was the conflation of the tasks of governing, commanding, and civilizing. In sub-Saharan Africa, colonization responded to the problems of establishing order and of producing the goods and objects it wanted. In this case, the form of sovereignty applied indiscriminately to people and objects; and the public domain proper constantly combined moral, economic, and political imperatives. In theory, arbitrary colonial power was intended to separate the political from the social and the moral, while at the same time closely connecting the three registers with the imperatives of production and profit. Improving the colonized peoples' condition and providing them with equipment and commercial or non-commercial goods was justified by the fact that they had to be integrated into the structures of production. For a long time, the chief means by which this integration was carried out was not free contractual arrangements, but rather coercion, violence, and corruption.

The different social policies tried out by successive administrations were moreover heavily determined by normative and disciplinary concerns. They sought to change the moral behavior of the colonized peoples. The vocabulary of the time put this under apparently different terms that were in reality interchangeable: "taming" (apprivoisement) and "training" (dressage). To carry on simultaneously these two tasks (controlling the natives and inserting them—in a potentially disruptive way—into the market

---

constitution of 1848, then abolished by decree on 2 February 1852, and finallyestablished by the republican constitution of 1875. On this question and on the preceding matters, see L. Deschamps, *Histoire de la question coloniale en France* (Paris: Librairie Plon, 1891).

order), command set up large-scale mechanisms of surveillance and an impressive arsenal of punishments and fines corresponding to a multiplicity of offenses. That is how we must understand the regulations regarding forced labor, obligatory crops, education, women, the family, marriage and sexuality, vagrancy, hygiene and prophylaxis, and even prison policy.[12] Within this formula of subjection, the colonized individual had no rights with respect to the state. A master-servant relationship bound him to the structure of power, the arsenal of paternalism not hesitating to express itself under the ideological mask of benevolence and the banner of humanism.

The social policies of postcolonial African regimes were also conceived on the basis of a view of the state that saw the latter as the organizer of public happiness. As such, the state allowed itself an opportunity to exercise an unlimited hold on each individual. But in practice, whether in the colonial period or after colonization, the state never played its exorbitant role wholly at the expense of society. Neither colonial command nor the postcolonial state succeeded in producing a total dislocation—and still less the disappearance—of all the bodies and all the lateral legitimacies that connected persons and groups locally. In order to facilitate their exchanges and to ensure the security of their property, social actors continued to resort to these lateral legitimacies and institutions, which they constantly reinvented, thereby providing them with new meanings and new functions.[13]

---

[12] Cf. the studies by J. Guyer, *Family and Farm in Southern Cameroon*, African Research Studies no. 15 (Boston: Boston University, 1984), 33-59; A. Isaacman and R. Roberts, eds., *Cotton, Colonialism and Social History in Sub-Saharan Africa* (London: James Currey, 1995), 147-179, 200-267; M. Vaughan, *Curing Their Ills: Colonial Power and African Illness* (Stanford: Stanford University Press, 1991).

[13] S. Berry, "Social Institutions and Access to Resources in African Agriculture," *Africa* 59 (1989): 41-55.

Contrary to some Western experiences, the extension of the powers of both the state and the market was thus not automatically founded on the rupture of the old social ties. In some cases, state domination—or the governmentalization of society—took place through the old hierarchies and the old networks of patronage. Two consequences of this process are worth mentioning. On the one hand, it opened the way, more than in other regions of the world, to an unprecedented privatization of public prerogatives. On the other, it allowed not only a degree of socialization of state power, which is generally poorly understood by analysts,[14] but also the socialization of arbitrary power that was its corollary—the two developments (the privatization of public prerogatives and the socialization of arbitrary state power) becoming, in this way, the very cement holding together postcolonial African forms of authoritarianism.

On the other hand, all through the nineteenth century and during the first half of the twentieth century, governing a colony meant first of all having command over the indigenes. "Civilization" first presented itself in its brutal form, in its battle-dress, through the very act of conquest, that is, the right to kill and to rely on force. Exercising command thus means requiring people to meet obligations. It also means, just as it does in the army, proceeding by injunctions, orders, and summonses. Command itself is simultaneously a tone, a mode of dress, and an attitude. Power comes down to the right to command, that is, to require, to force, to forbid, to oblige, to authorize, to subject, to punish, to recompense, to be obeyed—in short, to enjoin and to direct. The essence of colonial sovereignty is thus to administer orders and to have them carried out. The fourth characteristic of this kind of sovereignty

---

[14] This is the case for B. Badie, *L'État importé* (Paris: Fayard, 1993). For a rectification, see J. F. Bayart, "L'historicité de l'État importé," *Cahiers du CERI* (Paris, 1996).

is its circularity. The institutions it sets up for itself, the procedures it creates, the techniques it uses, and the knowledge on which it is based are not deployed with a view to achieving any particular public benefit. Their primary goal is absolute domination. The objective of this kind of sovereignty is to make people obey it. In this sense, and beyond ideological justifications, colonial sovereignty is circular.[15]

Precisely what is this form of government related to? Who is subjected to this kind of rationality and what course of human events is it supposed to govern? It is related, of course, to the territory that constitutes the colony. The colonial territory has its extent, its configuration, its boundaries. It has its geological makeup and its climates. It is endowed with resources. It has its soils, its minerals, its animal and plant species, its empty regions. In short, it has its qualities. But above all, there are the people who live there, their characters and customs (relating to marriages, successions, property, ways of alienating productive labor...), their manner of acting and thinking, their habits, the events they experience. These people, taken as a group, are those who were called indigenes. They constituted, so to speak, the raw material of government. They were to be bound in relationships of subjection that were first called "race policy" (politique des races) and later on "native policy" (politique indigène).[16] The latter explained how to handle this raw material, how to multiply it; what laws to impose on it, what punishment, suffering, and torture to inflict upon it; what labor and what services to demand of it; what satisfactions it should be

---

[15] M. Foucault, "La gouvernamentalité," *Magazine littéraire* no. 269 (1989): 101.

[16] See for example "La politique indigène du Gouverneur-Général Ponty en Afrique Occidentale Française," *Revue du Monde Musulman* 31 (1915); P. Meunier, *Organisation et fonctionnement de la justice indigène en Afrique Occidentale Française* (Paris, 1914); A. Girauld, *Principes de colonisation et de législation* (Paris, 1922). For an overview, see R. L. Buell, *The Native Problem in Africa* (New York: Macmillan, 1928), vols. 1-2.

denied; how to derive the maximum advantage from its labor and to what extent one should be concerned about its sustenance.[17]

These relationships of subjection were based on an *imaginaire* of the indigene and a set of beliefs concerning his identity.[18] From this point of view, the indigene was a simple creature who was not very ambitious and liked to let himself just be carried along by life. The extraordinary simplicity of his existence was said to be shown by his way of speaking: "no complicated sentence constructions; no tenses, modes, or persons in verbs; no gender or number in nouns and adjectives; no more than the minimum required to express himself: infinitives, substantives, adverbs, and adjectives set alongside each other in simple direct sentences."[19]

---

[17] Further information regarding the colonial mode of governance are found in T. Mitchell, *Colonizing Egypt*; C. Young, *The African Colonial State in Comparative Perspective*; P. Berman and J. Lonsdale, *Unhappy Valley*. This does not mean that the colonial project was always applied as such or produced the expected results. What interests us here is the epistemology of power itself, its rational principle, the categories that constitute its foundation.

[18] *Comparative Perspective*; P. Berman and J. Lonsdale, *Unhappy Valley*. This does not mean that the colonial project was always applied as such or produced the expected results. What interests us here is the epistemology of power itself, its rational principle, the categories that constitute its foundation.

[18] Strictly speaking, it is not a matter of kinds of knowledge but of families of images and representations, and a network of prejudices. In this sense, command as a way of exercising power was also a set of perceptions, a way of imagining the colonized subject and investing this image with a reality that thereby became objective, not because such a reality actually existed as it was described, but because action was based on and related to what was considered to be real. And through such action a material reality was eventually produced.

[19] E. Ferry, *La France en Afrique* (Paris: Armand Colin, 1905), 227.

According to this view, the indigene loved the place where he was born; he moved about easily, but always came back to live among his own people. He worked without haste, lacked foresight, used what the soil gave him without restraint, never giving a thought to building up a reserve for bad years. The indigene was also recognizable by his exuberance, the liveliness of his enjoyment of things, his quickness of movement, and his mind, which had an insatiable hunger for pride, plotting, and trickery. His temperament was characterized by natural laziness. Not knowing how to write, he noted nothing down. Thus, for example, he had only a vague idea of his own age, remembering no more than the great events that had affected him personally and violently (earthquakes, invasions, famines...). He remained a child overwhelmed by a longstanding atavism; he was incapable of thinking for himself and made no distinction between vice and virtue.

In that respect, he was free from the rules of humanity. His actions and attitudes were not regulated by any social protocol. Ultimately, he did not represent the type of the happy man that he had been imagined to be, his state of nature having been deformed by centuries of barbarism, pitiless wars, and slavery. Left to himself, he was defenseless against outside forces, against diseases and wild animals. The apparent tranquility of his life resulted, it was said, from his idleness and indolence, and especially from the lack of foresight that led him to enjoy the present without giving a thought to the future. Crude and animal-like, he was not the master of his instincts. He took pleasure in crushing the weak, destroying without purpose or reason. Quick to return to the most brutal excesses of animal life, he was incapable of resisting violence and could not, by himself, manage to make the long and difficult ascent toward the good and the beautiful.[20] Such was the "anthropology."

---

[20] This "anthropology" of the indigene is set forth in many works of the period. See, for example, A. Hovelacque, *Les nègres de l'Afrique sub-équatoriale* (Paris,

Taken together, the arguments set forth above reveal two things that were to be decisive with regard to the impact of these *imaginaires* on the way indigenes were administered—on what was called "the art of colonizing."[21] On a theoretical level, these arguments show that the colonial enterprise is first of all the execution of a right (which is not negotiated but arrogated) over men and objects. In the conquest phase, it is not only a matter of the right to strive toward a goal—acquiring the raw materials one needs and in turn requiring the purchase of the products that one manufactures, as Sarraut puts it.[22] Above all, it is a matter of the right "to use whatever means are necessary to achieve the goal."[23] Thus, proceeding in the mode of harvesting, the creation of useful goods consists, for example, in "purely and simply seizing, in the subjected domain, foodstuffs and spontaneous products," even if this means "destroying what bears them" in order to get them more quickly.[24] In this sense, such a sovereignty resembles the state of nature to the extent that it allows itself to do whatever it wishes to the disadvantage of anyone at all, and particularly the indigene. It can possess, use, and enjoy

---

1889); M. Delafosse, *Haut-Sénégal-Niger* (Paris, 1912), 2 vols.; L. Tauxier, *Le noir du Yatenga* (Paris, 1917); L. Marc, *Le pays Mossi* (Paris, 1909); Le Général Faidherbe, *Le Sénégal* (Paris, 1889); G. Angoulvant, *La pacification de la Côte d'Ivoire* (Paris, 1916).

[21] See J. Duval, *Les colonies et la politique coloniale de la France* (Paris: Arthus Bertrand), 445-77.

[22] A. Sarraut, *La mise en valeur des colonies françaises* (Paris: Payot, 1923), 84-85.

[23] T. Hobbes, *On the Citizen*. Ed. and trans. by Richard Tuck and Michael Silverthorne (New York: Cambridge University Press, 1998).

[24] To characterize this "policy of exhaustion," of despoliation, Sarraut resorts to an image: "The tree is cut down to get the fruit, and it is not replanted." What is taken away is not restored, he adds. Cf. Sarraut, *La mise en valeur des colonies françaises*, 85.

everything that pleases it, because it is the sole competent judge of what is good and what is truly useful for it, and because no matter what it does to the indigene it commits no offense against him. It is in this sense that we can say that it exercises absolute domination over the indigene.

But—and this is one of its paradoxes—this form of sovereignty, composed of possessiveness, injustice, and cruelty, also sees itself as bearing a "burden" that is nonetheless not a contract. In theory, colonial sovereignty does not ally itself with the object of command, that is, the indigene. In theory, no mutual need exists between the two parties. Neither is there any hope of a possible mutual good. On the contrary, colonial sovereignty is defined by the certainty of its omnipotence. Its right to rule and command must not in any case tolerate resistance on the part of the indigene. This form of government is not based on the idea of a pact, since, as Hobbes points out, "the matter or subject of a covenant is always something that falls under deliberation" (*Leviathan,* Part One, Chap. 14). Colonial sovereignty does not compromise regarding its rights. On the contrary, it divests its object and deprives it of what had formerly belonged to it.

Colonial sovereignty nonetheless presents itself as a free gift, intended to relieve its object of its wretchedness and to deliver it from its abject condition by elevating it to the rank of a human being. That is what A. Sarraut called "the right of the stronger to help the weaker." Colonial conquest, he explained, "is not the right but the fact of being stronger; the true right of the stronger is the generous right that he grants himself to succor, help, and protect the weaker, to be his guide and tutor."[25] The elevation of the indigene to a point where he can envisage the recovery of his rights

---

[25]   A. Sarraut, *La mise en valeur des colonies françaises*, 113.

23

is to be achieved by moral education. The latter's chief means is benevolence, and its goal is work.[26]

Benevolence is supposed to soften command. Work, for its part, is supposed to allow the creation of useful goods, produce values and wealth by overcoming scarcity and poverty. In addition, it is supposed to ensure the satisfaction of needs and the multiplication of pleasures.

The state that proceeds from this kind of sovereignty is defined as a protective state. The indigene is its protégé. The strength of this state resides both in the feeling that arises from the right to protect the weak and in the properly conceived pursuit of metropolitan profit. Its strength is a strength of good and benevolence. It is also a family-state. And it is in this measure that a "familial and filial tie binds the colonies to the mother country."[27] The protective state cannot, however, promote an abdication of the familial tutelage that it exercises over its "protégé," the indigene. The same goes for its sovereignty, that is, its moral superiority, the power of good that it provides the indigene as a free gift. The indigene, tied in a docile manner to family tutelage, could himself envisage his total freedom only at his own risk. An indigene (or a protégé) cannot, in fact, be a legal subject (sujet de droit). Authority having assigned him a sort of a minority that has no imaginable end, he cannot be a political subject—that is, a citizen.[28] Since the concept of a citizen coincides with that of

---

[26] "The black man does not yet understand the usefulness of work... To teach him how to work, to make him like work, to show him the material advantage he can derive from it, is to prepare his moral progress and to elevate him one rung up the ladder of humanity." In E. Ferry, 242.

[27] A. Sarraut, *La mise en valeur des colonies françaises*, 116. On the antecedents of this familial image, see L. Hunt, *The Family romance of the French Revolution* (Berkeley: University of California Press, 1992).

[28] P. Lampué and L. Rolland, *Précis de législation coloniale* (Paris: Dalloz, 1940).

nationality, the colonized individual who does not have the right to vote is not merely situated on the margins of the nation; he is virtually a stranger in his own land. The idea of political and civil equality, that is, of an equivalent status for all the inhabitants of the colony, is thus not what constitutes the social bond in this case. The notion of disobedience and domination in the colonies is based on the assertion that the state has no social debt with regard to the colonized people and that the latter can ask nothing of the state except what the state, in its benevolence, consents to grant to it and which it reserves, in any case, the right to withdraw at any time.

## Subjection and the Forms of Its Validation

As in colonial regimes, respect for legal subjects and individuals' freedom of action does not constitute the main characteristic of African governments whose crisis and collapse is taking place before our eyes. Is it necessary to recall that the juridical model of sovereignty does not allow us to account for the relationships of subjection as they functioned, even recently, in these states? In order to understand how these relations were established, it is important to go beyond the slogans fashionable in traditional political science (states that are weak, strong, patrimonial...) and reflect on the way in which the state sought to increase its value and to manage useful goods, whether in the context of scarcity or in the context of abundance. Following fashions that came from outside, many hasty observers have set out to conceptualize and describe these relationships and their overcoming by using, in a non-critical way, notions such as the relations between the state and "civil society"[29] or a "transition to democracy." Let us begin by examining the former notion; the latter will be dealt with in the second part of this study.

---

[29] Cf. most of the studies collected in J. Harbeson, et al., *Civil Society in Africa* (Boulder, CO: Lynne Rienner, 1994).

In the history of the West itself, the notion of civil society includes many different meanings. Moreover, these meanings vary from one period to another.[30] In lieu of elaborating an archaeology here, it will suffice for the moment to emphasize that the idea of civil society is inseparable from the—very ancient—reflection on the distinction between private and public seigniory, between "individual affairs" and "public affairs." It will be recalled, in fact, that until the eighteenth century people's general image of society was inseparable from their idea of the conflicts that divided different classes.

These conflicts did not arise solely from problems such as property (who has the right to use, to enjoy, and to dispose of what in an exclusive and absolute manner), successions (to whom should the patrimony left by a deceased person be transmitted), contracts (under what conditions the conventions, through which one or several persons obligate themselves to one or several others to do something, are valid) or civil status. They also have to do with the various forms taken by the relationships of enslavement and violence, as well as with the privileges derived from particular usurpations (what were called, at the time, feudal rights). The central issue thus becomes the means by which these conflicts of interest can be contained and arbitrated. It is in order to resolve such issues that theories of civil law arise and develop. Originally, the latter were concerned chiefly with murder and violent crimes of all kinds. But they soon included other domains as well. Thus it can be said that at the origin of civil society is violence, or at any rate,

---

[30]  For an overview, consult J. P. Duprat, "État et société civile de Hobbes à Hegel," *Cahiers Wilfredo Pareto* 20-21 (1982): 3225-48. See also C. Taylor's synthesis in "Modes of Civil Society," *Public Culture* 3 (1990): 99-118; J. Keane, ed., *Civil Society and the State: New European Perspectives* (London: Verso, 1988), 35-100; A. Arato and J. Cohen, *Civil Society* (Cambridge, MA: MIT Press, 1993).

the need to manage violence in such a way as to avoid situations in which each person is in a position to make war and to levy taxes, to arrogate public power to himself, and to exercise a relationship of domination based solely on the law of arbitrary power.

The idea that "individual affairs" must be separated from matters involving ecclesiastical power, or that matters of ecclesiastical power are not the same as matters of secular power—all this led to the establishment of laws, whose goal was on the one hand to destroy the power of customs, traditions, and authorities perceived as unjust and tyrannical, and on the other to guarantee the establishment of private freedom by distinguishing it from public sovereignty. It is in this context that the very notion of civility was shaped. It was opposed to barbarism and, by extension, to tyranny. In this sense, one can say that the idea of civil society arose from the debate concerning the relations between law and power, that is, in the way in which the juridical sphere was gradually delimited and its originality, peculiar value, and autonomy with respect to state absolutism were confirmed.

All these developments cannot simply be attributed to the philosophy of the Enlightenment and to the way in which it conceived eminently practical questions, such as those of the political constitution, freedom, inalienable and imprescriptible rights, the social contract, and the protection of property. The importance of the heritage of the Middle Ages is undeniable. For many medieval thinkers, society had within itself a principle of resistance to the invasive strength of political power. The latter itself was only one power among many others. Latin Christianity had taken up and refined this idea of differentiation, the Church presenting itself as an "independent society." The Augustinian principle of the existence of two cities (the earthly city and the City of God) opened the way to the possibility of conceptualizing the limitation of political power, if necessary by putting this limitation on a theological foundation. To all this, we must add the role played by particular aspects of medieval arrangements. For example, the latter provided for a series of obligations and rights for vassals. Vassals might enjoy these rights as a kind of property. A whole tradition of subjective rights thus developed in the shadow of serfdom. Other visible structures (for instance, relatively independent and self-governing cities) consolidated this *imaginaire* and contributed to its crystallization, and later on, to its formulation in a theoretical and juridical corpus.[31]

The critique of the state, law, and society, systematically pursued in the course of the eighteenth century, was accompanied by a critique of manners and vices. But discourses on virtue, the passions, and interests predated the century of Enlightenment proper.[32] According to Norbert Elias, civility is inseparable from court society and the transformations of the European absolutist state. Court society was characterized, among other things, by the conflation of public life and private life, the domain of the intimate and the secret, and by the distance it was necessary to maintain between the king and the nobility, the masters and their servants. More than the real attributes and advantages, the representation one could project determined in large measure the idea that other members of court society formed of each person's power and influence, as well as of his rank. Because of the restrictive character of public formalities and the importance of labels and ceremonials in the designation of ranks and hierarchies, the

---

[31]  Useful information on these aspects is found in J. Baechler, J. Hall, and M. Mann, eds., *Europe and the Rise of Capitalism* (London: Basil Blackwell, 1988). See also A. Ferguson, *An Essay on the History of Civil Society*, ed. Duncan Forbes (Edinburgh, 1966), 125-41 and 235-52.

[32]  See J. G. A. Pocock, *Virtue, Commerce, and History* (Cambridge: Cambridge University Press, 1991; A. O. Hirschman, *The Passions and the Interests: Political Arguments for Capitalism Before its Triumph* (Princeton: Princeton University Press, 1977; M. B. Becker, *Civility and Society in Western Europe, 1300-1600* (Bloomington: Indiana University Press, 1988).

competition for the signs of prestige was one of the central stakes in the competition among courtiers. These arrangements as a whole led to the reshaping of affectivity, since the respect for disciplines, the censorship of feelings, the mastery of spontaneous drives and immediate impulses was the cardinal rule of civility.[33]

Later on, the ideas of refinement, sociability, courtesy, and urbanity became established and circulated within the body social as a whole, thanks to the competition that drove bourgeois élites to imitate the manners of the court nobility. In order to renew the discriminating value of their behavior, and even to confiscate for its own advantage the symbolic advantages that were to be derived from it, the aristocracy increased the requirements of civility, multiplied prohibitions, and raised the level of censorship, thereby dramatizing the competition to appropriate the signs of distinction. Consequently, the transformation of behaviors, the respect for restrictive conventions, the supervision of conduct—in short, the promotion of less brutal relationships among people— are inseparable from the very concept of civil society. On the other hand, the latter points to the idea of a pacified and civilized society in which, the affections and passions having been mastered, self-control and the exchange of good manners gradually replace crude physical violence. Henceforth, the apparatus of domination and the modalities of enslavement are no longer forced to assume the appearance of the vulgar, summary force that characterized, for instance, the colonial regime.

From all the preceding, it follows that the idea of civil society points, even in the West, to particular forms of construction, legitimation, and

---

[33] N. Elias, *Court Society*, trans. E. Jephcott (Oxford: Basil Blackwell, 1983). For the rest, see the same author's *Power and Civility: The Civilizing Process*, trans. E. Jephcott (New York: Pantheon, 1982), 229-333.

conflict-resolution within the public sphere. But civil society is unthinkable apart from the existence of autonomous institutions and sites, of social coalitions capable of playing, if need be, the role of intermediaries between the state and society. Historically, civil society responded to the general problem of legitimating a domination that was otherwise seen as arbitrary, that is, as having no justification other than itself and to that end allowing itself to proceed without a normative acceptance on the part of the dominated peoples.[34]

Since the domination we are thinking of here (the concentration of violence, the exercise of constraint, the appropriation of products and food supplies, the allocation of useful goods, the judgment of lawsuits, the training of populations) is, among other things, the one exercised by the particular kind of institutional arrangement that is the state, it follows that its legitimation, that is, its normative acceptance by the dominated peoples, raises indirectly the problem of how to determine the limits of state power itself. As a result, there can be no civil society without a set of places and spaces where the ideas of autonomy, representation, and pluralism are crystallized, publicly, and where legal subjects are formed, who have rights and are capable of freeing themselves from arbitrary power, whether the latter is that of the state or that of the primary group (family, tribe…).

As it was problematized in the West, civil society is therefore not to be confused with the simple existence of autonomous associations developing outside state tutelage or with society itself (an error committed by several observers of Africa). In fact, the emergence of associations does not suffice to allow one automatically to conclude that a civil society exists.[35] The autonomy in question here does not

---

[34] See J. Leca, "La visite de la vieille dame," doc. pol., table ronde, Aix-en-Provence, October 1989, p. 4.

[35] A confusion widespread in the writings of analysts of eastern and central Europe

mean solely that a separate sphere is constituted outside or beyond the state.[36] It resides above all in the way in which the production and distribution of power are achieved through a plurality of independent sources and in the capacity of these sources to articulate, in full autonomy and within the public sphere, an idea of the general interest.[37] The process by which what is recognized as the "common" or "general" interest comes to be defined as such implies the existence of a public domain that it would be inappropriate to assimilate, simply and purely, to the official domain.

The notion of civil society refers, in addition, to a theory of social stratification and to procedures by means of which a minimum level of acceptance of this stratification can be established.[38] However, exclusion was not the main foundation of power's legitimacy. As J. Leca explains, what is critical is the tension—never resolved—between the reality of

---

and by their Africanist epigones. See, for example, J. Frentzel-Zagorska, "Civil Society in Poland and Hungary," *Soviet Studies* 42 (1990): 759-77; E. Hankiss, "'The Second Society.' Is there an Alternative Model Emerging in Contemporary Hungary?" *Social Research* 55 (1988), nos. 1-2; M. C. Hann, "Second Economy and Civil Society," *Journal of Communist Studies* 6 (1990): 21-44.

[36] See, for this kind of misunderstanding, M. Bratton's note, "Beyond the State: Civil Society and Associational Life in Africa," *World Politics* 41 (1989). Or the studies in D. Rothchild and N. Chazan, eds., *The Precarious Balance: State and Society in Africa* (Boulder, CO: Westview Press, 1988).

[37] On the different senses of the notion of "public" in European history, see J. Habermas, *The Structural Transformation of the Public Sphere: An Inquiry into a Category of Bourgeois Society*, trans. T. Burger (Cambridge, MA: MIT Press, 1989). For a recent critique of Habermas's views, see C. Calhoun, ed., *Habermas and the Public Sphere* (Cambridge, MA: MIT Press, 1993).

[38] Cf. J. L. Cohen, *Class and Civil Society: The Limits of Marxian Critical Theory* (Amherst, MA: University of Massachusetts Press, 1982).

31

inequality on the one hand, and on the other the fact that to be legitimate, power needs to be based on inclusion and equality, even if merely formal, among citizens. Thus one cannot pertinently apply this concept to postcolonial African configurations without taking seriously the set of connotations it suggests: the autochthonous categories that make it possible to conceive in political terms the relationship between conflict and violence, the privileged vocabularies in which the political imagination is formulated and the latter's institutional translations, the anthropology which subtends both questions of representation and questions concerning the inegalitarian allocation of useful goods, the negotiation of heterogeneity, and the polishing of the passions.

## Violence, Transfers, and Allocations

At this point we need to deal with a second series of arguments that claim to account for the process of decomposition in postcolonial African states. The notion is widespread that in sub-Saharan Africa, the state was no more than a simple structure imposed by violence on societies that were not only external to it but hostile to it as well.[39] To be sure, a large number of communities with very fragmented structures of power first experienced this in the colonial context. But in addition to the fact that state traditions existed in certain parts of the continent before the European conquest, it must be emphasized that not only state formulas, but also the colonial rationality outlined above were reappropriated early on by Africans.[40]

---

[39] Cf. G. Hyden, *No Shortcuts to Progress: African Development Management in Perspective* (Berkeley: University of California Press, 1983), or R. H. Jackson and C. G. Rosberg, "Why Africa's Weak States Persist: The Empirical and the Juridical in Statehood," *World Politics* 35 (1982): 1-24.

[40] This process is well documented in J. F. Bayart, *L'État en Afrique: La politique du ventre* (Paris: Fayard, 1989).

This reappropriation was not solely institutional in nature. It took place in the material domain and in the realm of the *imaginaire* as well.

As a result, both under colonization and after it, a constellation of properly autochthonous interests had been gradually forged. It played an eminent role in the transformation of ancestral systems of power and in the reconfiguration of alliances, including economic alliances, among the natives and the colonists. Particularly after the Second World War, these transformations eventuated in the creation, by Africans, of a relatively high number of small enterprises, at least in certain colonies. Most of these enterprises specialized either in commerce or in transportation.[41] Taking advantage of foreign firms' desire to control the native market, many African merchants succeeded in being entrusted with the distribution of various products, thus occupying positions intermediary between the colonial firms and local consumers.[42]

In a parallel manner, important restructurations had taken place in the domain of cash-crop agriculture (cocoa, coffee, cotton, peanuts...). A stratum of relatively well-off planters was thus growing up in rural areas. Its role—whether as a social base, a supporting power, or an opposition—was decisive in the emergence of anticolonialist feeling and in the forms later taken on by nationalist movements.[43] Sometimes in competition with enlightened groups and with groups coming from the colonial

---

[41] See, for example, J. L. Dongmo, *Le dynamisme bamiléké* (Yaoundé: CEPER, 1981).

[42] See G. Kitching's remarks in his *Class and Economic Change in Kenya: The Making of an African Petite-Bourgeoisie* (New Haven: Yale University Press, 1980), 159-199.

[43] Cf. the examples reported in R. A. Joseph, *Le mouvement nationaliste au Cameroun: Les origines sociales de l'UPC* (Paris: Karthala, 1986).

bureaucracy, sometimes in symbiosis with them, this constellation of interests greatly influenced the shaping of independent states. This was particularly the case when these states began to seek to set up the institutional mechanisms that were supposed to allow them to establish themselves in village communities (the creation of the basic organs of single parties, cooperatives, companies that were supposed to be concerned with development and the commercialization of cash crops, and various forms of territorial networks). It was in this way that the co-optation of the old élites and the launching of new intermediaries between the state, society, and the market were carried out. And it was also in this way that relationships of subjection were established and consolidated, which, even when their announced purpose was to move beyond them, to a large extent, prolonged relationships the colonial state had initiated.[44]

It thus turns out that in their recent form, African state entities—at the same time as they participated in a political universal—were built upon eminently autochthonous social foundations. Naturally, these social foundations varied from one country to another, from one region of the continent to another, and sometimes within a single country.[45] Moreover, a consistent interpretation of this local establishment can hardly fail to take into account the connections these different apparatuses (and the political forces that controlled them) simultaneously maintained with the international system. In certain cases, these international connections and local forms of social regulation were made possible by the exploitation of a favored mineral resource (diamonds in Sierra Leone,

---

[44] On a few aspects of this discussion, see P. Geschiere, *Village Communities and the State: Changing Relations among the Maka of Southeastern Cameroun since the Colonial Conquest* (London: Kegan Paul International, 1982).

[45] Cf., for example, J. F. Bayart, *L'État au Cameroun* (Paris: Presses de la Fondation nationale des science politiques, 1977).

uranium in Niger, copper in Zambia). In others, cash-crop agriculture constituted the material basis of public power. This was the case, not only in regions where a single product (such as peanuts in Sénégal or cotton in Chad) exercised its "dictatorship" over social and commercial exchanges as a whole,[46] but also where the combination of cash-crop agriculture, agricultural-industrial exportation, and a range of small industrial units had given rise to the beginnings of diversification (as in the Ivory Coast, Kenya, Zimbabwe, and, to a lesser extent, in Cameroon).

In still other cases, the intensive exploitation of a rare resource served— at least in certain periods—as the driving force behind increasing inequalities, the expansion of state power and prestige, and the distribution of useful goods. This was the case for oil in Nigeria in the 1970s.[47] Some other states combined the exploitation of agricultural resources (tropical woods, cocoa, coffee, palm oil, bananas, tobacco, tea) and underground resources (iron, copper, manganese, cobalt, oil) to set up more or less viable systems of inequality and domination (Cameroon, Gabon, Ivory Coast, Zimbabwe) or to pursue prolonged wars, waging war becoming the very source of the state's formation or destruction (as in Angola).

Whether they benefited from a single main resource or several resources, or were financed by their peasants, whether they were "assisted" or fell into debt, the modalities in which Africa was integrated into the world market broadly influenced the forms taken by postcolonial states and the way in which the élites in power inserted themselves into international

---

[46]  J. Copans, *Les marabouts de l'arachide* (Paris: L'Harmattan, 1989); D. Cruise O'Brien, *Saints and Politicians: Essays in the Organization of a Senegalese Peasant Society* (Oxford: Clarendon Press, 1975); M. Coumba Diop, ed., *Sénégal: trajectoires d'un État* (Dakar: CODESRIA, 1992).

[47]  R. A. Joseph, *Democracy and Prebendal Politics in Nigeria: The Rise and Fall of the Second Republic* (Cambridge: Cambridge University Press, 1988).

fields of activity. The income derived from these transactions in fact contributed (1) to the structuring of local systems of inequality and domination; (2) to the establishment of coalitions or the exacerbation of factional struggles; (3) to the determination of the types of external support from which these élites benefited. The forms of local exploitation of the work force (systems of taxation, the level of deductions...)— in short, the structuring of the relationships between the state, the market, and society— also depended on the modalities of this insertion into global trade. As had happened earlier in precolonial long-distance trade, it was chiefly thanks to the revenues drawn from this trade that that the relationships of subjection could be financed, scarcity avoided, values created, useful goods consumed, and ultimately, a process of "indigenizing" the state carried out. It is necessary to take these material factors into account if the contrasts observed today in the processes of public power's evanescence in Africa are not only to be intelligible on the internal level, but also to become the object of pertinent comparisons.

However, although the trajectories of the state's "indigenization" have varied from one country to another, the crystallization of the state and the *imaginaire* that supported it were everywhere achieved in an authoritarian fashion that denied individuals any status as legal subjects. This does not mean either that state domination was total and without concessions, or that those who held power enjoyed complete autonomy and were not exposed to pressure. As in colonial regimes, and as later in the communist regimes from which postcolonial states borrowed a certain number of their predicates, there in fact existed both formal and informal channels through which the circulation of élites took place. There were also sites in which the diverse local, ethnic, and regional interests were negotiated, arbitration carried out, and a degree of social control achieved.[48]

---

[48]  On the communist regimes, see G. Gleason, "Fealty and Loyalty: Informal

In all these countries, however, the act that established sovereign authority at no time constituted a genuine pact or contract, since strictly speaking, it did not imply any reciprocity of legally codified obligations between, on the one hand, the state and those who held power, and on the other hand, society and individuals. To be sure, one should avoid explaining everything by coercion. Similarly, one should avoid oversimplifying the various forms taken by state control and by the market's penetration of the various regions of sub-Saharan Africa since 1960. In some cases the beginnings of a transition from direct coercion to more internalized forms of control is observable. The practice of power has nonetheless been generally situated within a continuation of colonial political culture and of the most despotic aspects of ancestral traditions, which were reinvented for the purpose.[49] That is one of the reasons why postcolonial sovereignty was hostile to public debate, and why its criteria of judgment and action gave little weight to the distinction between the justified and the arbitrary. Because it no longer had any source outside itself, sovereignty arrogated the right to "command." It is true that this kind of right to "command" sought to legitimate itself by appealing to various sources, simultaneously utilizing the ancestral *imaginaires* and imported *imaginaires*.[50] But it was rarely the counterpart

---

Authority Structures in Soviet Asia." *Soviet Sudies*, 43, 4, 1991, pp. 613-628. See also M. Urban, "Centralisation and Elite Circulation in a Soviet Republic," *British Journal of Political Science*, 19, 1, 1989.

[49] Cf. the examples reported by D. Bigo, *Pouvoir et obéissance en Centrafrique* (Paris: Karthala, 1989; C. Toulabor, *Le Togo sous Eyadéma* (Paris: Karthala, 1986); and T. M. Callaghy, "Culture and Politics in Zaire," doc. pol., October 1986.

[50] See, on this aspect, M. G. Schatzberg, "Power, Language and Legitimacy in Africa," a paper presented at the Conference on "Identity, Rationality, and the Postcolonial Subject: African Perspectives on Contemporary Social Theory," Columbia University, New York, February 28, 1991.

of a duty—constitutionally recognized and defended as such—to protect (whether individuals, their property, their private rights, or their physical and bodily integrity).

Wherever material and alimentary inducements were not sufficient to produce unconditional submission, "spontaneous" obedience, or expressions of "gratitude" on the part of subjected peoples, massive resort was taken to public coercion.[51] Whatever the scope of the abuses committed by those in power, nothing relieved subjected peoples of the obligation to submit, not even elections.[52] Thus, almost everywhere in sub-Saharan Africa, the practical distinction between the tasks of conducting public affairs properly so-called (government) and the unrestricted, institutional use of violence and coercion was virtually nonexistent.[53] The mechanisms of the deployment of violence and the means of punishment were systematically exploited, whether to repress dissidence, to crush rebellions, to silence protests, or simply to seize power.[54] It was often a matter of "commanding," and not necessarily one of "governing."

---

[51] Cf. T. M. Callaghy, "Police in Early Modern States: The Uses of Coercion in Zaire in Contemporary Perspective," a paper given at the American Political Science Association meeting, Denver, Colorado, 1982.

[52] See again T. M. Callaghy, "State-Subject Communication in Zaire," *The Journal of Modern African Studies* 18 (1981): 469-492.

[53] M. G. Schatzberg, *The Dialectics of Oppression in Zaire* (Bloomington: Indiana University Press, 1988), 30-70. See also "Violence et pouvoir," a special issue of the journal *Politique africaine* 42 (1991).

[54] P. McGowan and T. A. Johnson, "African Military Coups d'État and Underdevelopment: A Quantitative Historical Analysis," *Journal of Modern African Studies* 22 (1984): 633-666.

The consequences of such practices had a decisive influence on the forms taken, in these various countries, by the current efforts to move beyond authoritarianism. It goes without saying that such moves did not signify an automatic transition toward democracy, but on the contrary could lead to various forms of chaos or hidden anarchy. The authoritarian *imaginaire* thus consolidated in the period of colonial occupation and independence, also had a considerable influence on the way in which social movements emerged, the framework within which they were deployed, the forms of mobilization they promoted, their chances of victory and the possibilities of defeating them. To assess the influence of this *imaginaire* properly, it does not suffice to mention the legends of personal rule, of the "big man" or patrimonial power, as has been customarily done. It is important to examine the connections that postcolonial power had woven between the production of violence and the systems of allocating food supplies and gifts. If from the economic point of view, the administration of violence and the exercise of raw power rarely served to organize the production of wealth in an effective manner, at least at the end of the 1970s one could credit a certain number of postcolonial systems of inequality and domination with a certain efficacity in allocating useful goods and pleasures.

In order to carry out this allocation, efforts had been made, as in certain Arab countries, to transform wherever possible the institutions of society and even corporate bodies into intermediaries of power. Whence the "governmentalization" (caporalisation) of labor unions, the regimentation of the churches, the co-optation of associations of various kinds, the colonization of tribal lands and other so-called customary institutions.[55]

---

[55] On the Arab world, see G. Salamé, "Sur la causalité d'un manque: pourquoi le monde arabe n'est-il donc pas démocratique?", *Revue française de science politique*, 41, 3, 1991.

The state might also control ethnic and regional tensions, by resorting to the creation of jobs in the public sector, to deficit financing, or to direct intervention in the system of production. The choices made concerning production, investment, allocation of bank credits and titles to real estate, the granting of public works contracts, the regulation of import-export trade, public consumption, the administration of prices and systems of subsidy, the granting of licenses and other authorizations, the control of trade, customs, and taxation procedures, the management of interactions between urban and rural areas and between industry and agriculture—in short, financial balancing and the very definition of political economics, were not necessarily (or at least not exclusively) governed by either the imperatives of competitiveness or an effective concern about profits.

Although these aspects were not systematically ignored in the calculations of African decision-makers, we should note that in addition to ensuring a substantial number of individuals the various kinds of useful goods that were absolutely necessary for their survival, the state's assumption of direct responsibility for productive activities was also intended to lead to a political advantage, insofar as it was indirectly intended to affect the circuits of regional redistribution (the assignment of equipment and infrastructures, the development of revenues, schools), the training of workers, the constitution of clienteles and the consolidation of networks of patronage. It is these two imperatives (the provision of useful goods indispensable for survival and political advantage) that explain, in part, the proliferation of public and parapublic mechanisms, the politics of recruitment, attribution of advantages, salaries, and bonuses.[56]

---

[56]  B. Contamin and Y. A. Fauré, *La bataille des entreprises publiques en Côte d'Ivoire: l'histoire d'un ajustement interne* (Paris: Karthala, 1990), 179-239.

Taken as a whole, these political-economic mechanisms also made possible the maintenance of a complex system of transferring revenues from formal and official circuits to parallel circuits, from urban homes to rural homes, from the richest to the poorest.[57] These transfers of revenues (aid to families, social spending and various benefits such as subsidies to defray the costs of funerals, schooling, and healthcare, participation in so-called customary ceremonies, various forms of contributions, the purchase of titles and medals...) were themselves amplified by a social ethic that, while granting a large role to individualism, attributed central functions to redistribution and imposed duties and obligations on those with large fortunes, in conformity with the status to which they aspired, even if the costs thus incurred often far surpassed their real revenues.[58] In a still more decisive way, the modalities in which these political-economic mechanisms functioned depended on the shapes taken by both social stratification and the internal relationships of power among groups and ethnic units. In a word, by partially or completely substituting itself for the market, the state became a prodigious machine for creating and regulating inequalities.

Postcolonial sovereignty was thus in itself a formula for domination, which, while participating in universal technologies (a state and its mechanisms), had its own internal coherence and rationality in the domains of politics, economics,

---

[57] For an illustration of this, cf. M. Russel, "Beyond Remittances: The Redistribution of Cash in Swazi Society," *The Journal of Modern African Studies* 22 (1984): 595-615.

[58] See F. R. Mahieu, "Principes économiques et société africaine," *Tiers monde* 30 (1989); J. I. Guyer, ed., *Money Matters: Instability, Values and Social Payments in the Modern History of West African Communities* (Portsmouth NH: Heinemann, 1993).

and the *imaginaire*.[59] Hence it must be evaluated in relation to this peculiar rationality, and not on the basis of an ideal and normative Weberian model that does not exist anywhere in the real world. We can account for neither postcolonial sovereignty's own economic and political (in)coherence, nor for its trajectories of implosion if we limit ourselves to an analysis solely in terms of monetary orthodoxy. We must examine the failures registered within the triptych that constituted the very foundation of postcolonial African forms of authoritarianism. We have already discussed violence at some length. Let us now examine briefly the two other dimensions of this triptych.

First, there was an allocation of a purely statist type. This allocation was granted in two forms. First, salary. It is important to linger on this a moment, in order to make explicit the relationships between salary and the constitution of the dominated subject.[60] In theory a salary is a remuneration one receives in return for work done, for a service or benefit rendered. By "work" we must understand both the time and the effort devoted to the production of something "useful." We can also consider the work itself and the product that results from it as a kind of "merchandise" sold to a buyer at a profit. During the authoritarian period, there was no automatic relationship either between work (its quantity and value) and salary or between the salary one received, the useful goods one produced, and the general wealth that resulted.

On the one hand, one could enrich oneself without having to endure fatigue and hunger (what we have called suffering). On the other hand, one could devote one's time to the production of perfectly useless things

---

[59] Cf. N. Caswell, "Autopsie de l'ONCAD: la politique arachidière au Sénégal, 1966-1980," *Politique africaine* 14, 39-73.

[60] The following developments are drawn from a study by A. Mbembe, J. Roitman, "Figures of the Subject in Times of Crisis," *Public Culture* 5 (1995).

or, in any case, that in no way contributed to the formation of general wealth. In this context, a salary's primary function was not to reward productivity. It constituted, above all, an allocation of a purely ascriptive nature.[61] Since the enjoyment of a salary almost always involved more than the individual who received it, salary as an institution was a essential part of the dynamics of the relationships between state and society. It served as a resource, allowing the state to purchase obedience and gratitude and to bind the population to disciplinary apparatuses. In other terms, a salary was what legitimated not only subjection, but also the development of a type of political exchange based not on the principle of political equality and the associated representation, but on the existence of obligations by means of which the state fabricated liens on society, the construction of the relationship of subjection being achieved in the distributive order and not in the order of equivalence among human persons endowed with their own natural and civil rights and therefore able to play a role in political decisions. The state transformed salaries into obligations, and all those to whom it granted subsistence incomes became its debtors. At the same time, the only people who had salaries were those who were dependents of the state. The subsistence income they received did not reward the conversion of energy into wealth. Instead, it had the effect of outlining a particular figure of obedience and domination. That is the reason why in certain public discourses these debts were treated, if not as favors, at least as privileges.

The other forms of state allocation were developed in connection with a way of regulating the political order that was based in large measure on the private appropriation of public resources with a view to constructing

---

[61] These remarks apply first of all to bureaucratic work. For the rest, see for example the studies collected by M. Agier, et al., *Classes ouvrières d'Afrique noire* (Paris: Karthala, 1987), 45-76; 141-181; 215-245.

43

allegiances.[62] This kind of political order had been able to crystallize and function viably on two conditions. On the one hand, there was a predatory economy based on three elements: debt, spending, and deficit. On the other, a general system of privileges and impunity made it possible to ensure the latter's reproduction on a relatively enlarged scale. The appropriation of public resources and the privatization of the state took various forms. First, there were the privileges and preferential treatment that those who held positions of authority granted themselves, and whose cumulative value went beyond—sometimes far beyond—the salary itself: lodging, furnishings, water, electricity, cars, servants, costs for reception and representation, bonuses, reserve funds. Then there was the whole system of parallel payments (embezzlement): the double payment of rents, fictitious administrative leases, hidden commissions, bribes and overbillings connected with public works contracts, the allocation of titles to real estate, and customs and taxation procedures. Finally, there were parallel tax levies connected with the ebb and flow of the state's finances. All the way down to the lower levels of administration, public services were for sale. This was the case, for instance, when official stamps were put on documents and visas and when they were issued. It was also the case when motorists were stopped

---

[62]  That is what some authors have called the mode of clientelist and patrimonial redistribution. See in particular J. F. Médard, "The Underdeveloped State in Tropical Africa: Political Clientelism or Neo-Patrimonialism?," in C. Clapham, ed., *Private Patronage and Public Power: Political Clientelism in the Modern State* (London: Frances Pinter, 1983). On a related subject, see R. A. Joseph, *Democracy and Prebendal Politics in Nigeria* (Cambridge: Cambridge University Press, 1989). For a different way of theorizing these phenomena, see J. F. Bayart, *L'État en Afrique: La politique du ventre* (Paris: Fayard, 1989). A few examples of the practices to which these theories refer are found in B. Contamin and Y.-A. Fauré, *La bataille des entreprises publiques en Côte-d'Ivoire: L'histoire d'un ajustement interne* (Paris: Karthala, 1990), 219-230.

for routine inspections and when licenses and other authorizations were granted.[63]

Thanks to these two forms of allocation, economic matters were converted into social and political ones. It was through their mediation that a great many people conceived an idea of "the good life" and succeeded in surmounting material scarcity—or were simply freed of the terror arising from insecurity, poverty, and lack. In a more decisive way, it is thanks to these forms of allocation that the triple process involving the governmentalization (étatisation) of society, the socialization of state power, and the privatization of public prerogatives was achieved: these three phases constituted, as we have already pointed out, the very cement holding together postcolonial African forms of authoritarianism. But to understand the socialization of arbitrary power inherent in these three phases, we must now examine the logic of transfers.

The most widespread form of transfer was the communitarian social bond.[64] This refers to a complex system of reciprocities and obligations connecting the members of a single household or a single community. For example, these obligations and reciprocities related, within a vast

---

[63] Cf. A. Morice, "Guinée 1985. État, corruption, et trafics," *Les Temps modernes*, no. 487 (1987): 109-136. See also R. Tangri, "Servir ou se servir? À propos de Sierra Leone," *Politique africaine* 6 (1982): 5-18.

[64] Cf. F. R. Mahieu's synthesis, *Les fondements de la crise économique en Afrique: Entre la pression communautaire et le marché international* (Paris: L'Harmattan, 1990), 31-92. See also L. Glazier, *Land and the Uses of Tradition Among the Mbeere of Kenya* (New York: University Press of America, 1985); S. Berry, *No Condition is Permanent: The Social Dynamics of Agrarian Change in sub-Saharan Africa* (Madison: University of Wisconsin Press, 1993); J. Guyer, "Household and Community in African Studies," *African Studies Review* 24 (1981: 87-137.

field of regulated interactions, craftsman and apprentice, parent and child, man, woman, and mistress, young and old, youngest and eldest son, nephew and uncle, niece and aunt, lender and donor, protégé and patron, foreign worker and host.[65] These interactions, with their multiple ramifications, affected domains as diverse as the mutual transfers of time and goods, of labor and revenues. It was in this context that an important part of the revenues were, for example, transferred from the city to the countryside, thanks to visits involving help for family members, requests for help, contributions to the funeral rites for a close relative or fellow worker (burial, seventh-day celebrations, wakes), or regular contributions to insurance funds for people born in the area, to development associations or associations connected with the professional field, and to tontines. The reception, whether temporary or long-term, of relatives and close friends who were not part of the immediate household not only entailed providing lodging and food, but could also include gifts of money or paying the costs of educating the youngest children.

These interactions and the expenses that were their corollary functioned as a kind of social tax or an endless, multiform social debt owed to the community. The philosophy subtending this social tax was based on the principle that each individual was indebted to a collective patrimony that was not only financial but also included knowledge, techniques, and, in short, the material and identity-producing substructure, without which the individual, left to himself, would be unable to undertake

---

[65] On this last point, see J. M. Gastellu's analyses in *Riches paysans de Côte-d'Ivoire* (Paris: L'Harmattan, 1989). For the rest, consult anthropological works on families and the economy: M. Abeles, et al., *Âge, pouvoir et société en Afrique noire* (Paris: Karthala, 1985); F. Sabelli, *Le pouvoir des lignages en Afrique* (Paris: L'Harmattan, 1986); C. Vidal, *Sociologie des passions* (Paris: Karthala, 1991), 87-98, 161-178.

anything at all. It was thought that the moral security of the whole society, its common strength, depended on each person's contribution to this patrimony. The social debt preceded, as it were, each individual existence. It applied to everyone in relation to what fate had reserved for him. Not repaying it amounted to fracturing the community and to imperiling its chances of development. As a result, a person who tried to avoid repaying it without having some good reason for doing so ran the risk of social death. This was, for example, one of the meanings of the battles carried on through sorcery.

Paying this tax or debt at the same time involved putting others in one's debt, emphasizing one's claims on them: "expressions of gratitude on the part of the child whom one has supported in his studies and who, once he has succeeded, will be expected to help his parents, his younger brothers, the elderly members of his extended family, and, especially if he has managed to get a good position, the whole of his native community (his lineage, his village); to intervene on behalf of a son when he is indebted to the father; to lodge a young village boy when he is seeking employment in town; to contribute to the financing of a project to modernize the village; to make ostentatious donations to the funeral rites that are organized there to show his success, to honor the deceased person's family, and to thank the ancestors whom the deceased person has gone to rejoin…"[66]

It is important to stress that these interactions were not without conflicts. They were connected with an image of success and social prestige as well as with a concept of the responsibilities obtaining among age groups, sexes, and generations. They were not limited to the domains of the

---

[66] A. Marie, "'Y a pas l'argent': L'endetté insolvable et le créancier floué, deux figures complémentaires de la pauvreté abidjanaise," *Revue Tiers Monde* 36 (1995): 305-6.

household or family relations. They also covered, in various forms, the workplace and the religious community. In so doing, they helped constitute both the public and the private spheres. Thus a genuine system of social complicity was involved whose functioning made possible a special kind of domination founded on very personalized relationships and on the power to distribute and protect. This system was in no way supported by juridical texts. It was based on a variety of arrangements and customary rules, in short, on a complex of interiorized norms that defined, in the last analysis, the legitimate modalities of subjection and social control, whether in the framework of clientele relationships, family relationships, or broader systems of alliances.

It was in this way that the reproduction of each of these was achieved. Still more important, it was in this way that a general right was formed— informal and unwritten, however—to protection, security, and assistance. Each member of the community could claim this right and benefit from it, on the condition that he met the relevant norms. The right to receive help in case of an accident, sudden death, illness or other decline in status was manifested in the assistance that those who were better situated on the social scale owed to those who were not. This assistance was as regularly given as was required by the unforeseeable events of life and as the availability of time, money, and other non-monetary goods allowed.

However, we must observe that the triptych of violence, allocations, and transfers took very different forms, depending on the country, productive structures, and conditions affecting local and global markets.[67] In some contexts, it made it possible to stabilize institutions, to grant a certain legitimacy to established regimes, and to diminish the

---

[67] R. Bates, *Markets and States in Tropical Africa: The Political Basis of Agricultural Policies* (Berkeley: University of California Press, 1981).

risks of implosion.[68] This does not in any way mean that the conflicts regarding the distribution of revenues derived from duties on exports had ceased. On the contrary, they flared up, especially when the availability of funds increased following the rise in export receipts or when the amount of foreign credits became significantly larger. But in such cases, those in power had sufficient resources to deal with these conflicts, and this made systematic recourse to summary and disproportionate violence unnecessary.

The stability thus achieved, and then apparently strengthened by means of institutions that recruited and governmentalized society (a single party, single labor unions, associations of young people and women in the party, claques entrusted with orchestrating the cult of personality...), was nonetheless illusory, or in any case came at a high price. Since in economic terms, all that was required was a rebellion in world markets, to produce a fiscal crisis, which would prevent the state from making large numbers of gifts. That is what happened in the Ivory Coast and, to a lesser extent, in Cameroon and in Kenya. In fact, thanks to various kinds of private income, the regimes in power in these countries succeeded, in the 1970s, in enlarging their bases of support, especially among the "middle classes."[69] At the beginning of the 1980s, with the help of the economic recession, products and foodstuffs declined at an

---

[68]  For examples, consult J. R. Fletcher, "The Political Uses of Agricultural Markets in Zambia," *Journal of Modern African Studies* 24 (1986): 603-618, or N. Caswell, "Autopsie de l'ONCAD: La politique arachidière au Sénégal, 1966-1980," *Politique africaine* 14 (1984).

[69]  Data on these developments will be found in Y. A. Fauré and J. F. Médard, eds., *État et bourgeoisie en Côte d'Ivoire* (Paris: Karthala, 1982) and P. Geschiere and P. Konings, eds., *Proceedings of the Conference on the Political Economy of Cameroon: Historical Perspectives* (Leiden: Afrika Studie Centrum, 1989).

accelerated rate at the same time as the erosion of external financial reserves grew. Then there occurred a gradual estrangement of certain groups that, having profited from the previous arrangements, had succeeded in amassing personal fortunes or in acquiring small or middling amounts of property (high officials, high military officers, businessmen, teachers, journalists, lawyers...). Today, some of them promote dissidence. The arrangement of interests within the factions in power having prevented creative responses to such blockages, these regimes are currently bogged down in serious crises, which not only affect the institution of the state as such, but also threaten to rot away the whole social fabric.

In other contexts, redistribution took a frivolous and predatory form whose main effects were the depletion of public financial resources, a radical depreciation of the currency, an unprecedented fluctuation in prices, the degradation of institutions, and the decline of public authority. At the highest levels of the state in Zaire, in Somalia, in Sierra Leone, and in Liberia, for example, the allocation of useful goods and foodstuffs took the form of a virtually uncontrolled extension of the series of privileges, materials, advantages, and benefits that the clique in power allowed itself. On the cultural level, the things necessary for life, pleasures, and imaginary values had become completely confused. Within the ruling classes, the line of demarcation between luxury and caprice had disappeared. Contraband and speculation in currency guaranteed, in many cases, enormous profits.[70] At almost every intermediary level of administration, bureaucrats proceeded to skim large sums from the tide of official finances, thereby increasing fiscal disarray and budgetary problems. At the lower levels, an unprecedented practice

---

[70] J. MacGaffey, *Entrepreneurs and Parasites: The Struggle for Indigenous Capitalism in Zaïre* (Cambridge: Cambridge University Press, 1988).

of selling public services (issuance of documents, stamps, signatures, authorizations, certificates, licenses) had ended up subordinating the very activity of governing to the principle of venality.[71]

In addition, since the beginning of the 1970s most of these countries had entered a phase in which, from the legal and fiscal point of view, most of the national wealth had practically become part of the "eminent domain" of a tyrant acting as a mercenary with regard to the funds in the national treasury. Inextricable networks of interests and profits had been woven between, on the one hand, the merchants, money-lenders, and native financiers engaged in contraband and speculative operations, and on the other, those who held administrative and political power and international brokers—when the functions of both groups were not interconnected. In a parallel manner, the services entrusted with administering violence (the police, the army, presidential brigades, private militias...) had gradually increased in autonomy, when the gaps separating the upper hierarchy and the foot-soldiers had not grown larger.

The internal enclosure of the armed forces and the dispersion of the means of violence that had resulted from it had promoted, among lower-ranking soldiers and paramilitary forces, the emergence of modes of survival behavior that often adopted para-criminal methods: racketeering, murders, violent confiscations of property, and frequently genuine massacres.[72] This tendency had also affected the modalities of intervention on the part of the agents of the state and their brokers in operations of amassing wealth, whether in the formal sector or in the hidden sectors. When they are not torn apart by bloody civil wars,

---

[71]  C. Newbury, "Dead and Buried, or Just Underground? The Privatization of the State in Zaïre," *Canadian Journal of African Studies* 18 (1984).

[72]  See "Les massacres de Katekelay et de Luamuela," *Politique africaine* 6 (1982): 72-106.

these countries now find themselves in situations in which recourse to brute force has become the rule, whether in transactions between what remains of the state and individuals, or in ordinary social relations.

Where war has been avoided, chaos is developing, the implosion taking the form of a generalized social delinquency. This delinquency feeds on a culture of raiding and despoliation. In underprivileged groups, the enjoyment of "economic rights" henceforth consists in access to the most necessary food supplies. The continual erosion of the conditions of life is now accompanied by war, illness, and epidemics. The result of this combination is the aggravation of civil dissensions, increasingly frequent recourse to forms of mobilization based on ethnic, regional, or religious groups, and a frightening increase in the chances of dying a violent death.

The latter occurs, for example, in connection with public disorders and seditions. Popular protest increasingly takes the form of urban riots that lead nowhere. From time to time, mutinies break out. Armed soldiers occupy strategic positions in the capital city, demanding payment of back salaries. Where possible, they seize the treasury and empty it before going on to pillage, wreck, and rob shops, and to burn houses, cars, and other things. Sometimes they are joined by bands of looters and young men at a loose end.

Still more important, economic activity is increasingly related to military activity. The cutting of roads, the capture of loads of freight, escorts for convoys, and security services that can be rented all show that the boundaries between production, extortion, and predation have become blurred. It is no longer clear what belongs to whom or who has a right to what, and still less who should be excluded and on what basis. Institutional violence and the rioter's logic of pillage have as immediate consequence the prevention of any effective consolidation of so-called civil society while at the same time confining the state to impotence.

On the other hand, in configurations where the predatory fury characteristic of the first phase of colonization has been more or less contained, it is this elasticity in the redistribution of useful goods that in part grounded the legitimacy of postcolonial formulas of government, and made the relationships of inequality and coercion tolerable. This does not mean that inequalities and abuses were passively accepted, or that faced with arbitrary state power, the only possible response was resignation.[73] Taking into account the forms assumed by economic relationships and the circulation of products and foodstuffs, as well as the way in which economic relationships were articulated in a system of social stratification, political battles took on very unusual shapes (escape, evasion, dissimulation, dodges, derision, various kinds of lack of discipline and indocility) and expressed themselves in dynamic metaphors (family relationships, genealogy, memory and oblivion, sorcery, healing, dissidences of a religious origin...). It would be a mistake to confuse these social movements with other forms of struggle characteristic of situations in which the logics of the market have substantially impregnated social relationships.[74] However that may be, it can be said that in the African countries that were, until recently, considered the most "stable" and the most "prosperous" (Cameroon, Ivory Coast, Kenya, Gabon, Zimbabwe), a sort of "compromise" guaranteeing the welfare of the middle classes and the administrative

---

[73] See J. F. Bayart, A. Mbembe, and C. Toulabor, *Le politique par le bas en Afrique noire* (Paris: Karthala, 1992).

[74] On this subject, cf. Desjeux, *Stratégies paysannes en Afrique noire: Essai sur la gestion de l'incertitude* (Paris: L'Harmattan, 1987).

53

élites made it possible to ensure the postcolonial state's viability and to endow it with authentically indigenous roots.

Thanks to this compromise, those in power could dip heavily into the agricultural surpluses and petroleum and mining revenues. Accompanied by the exercise of coercion and an often summary administration of violence, these levies made it possible to purchase loyalties and to compel allegiances, generally at a high cost. The fluidity between the economic and commercial spheres and the political and administrative spheres, the lack of a distinction between public wealth and private property, and the osmosis between private economic agents (national and foreign) and local holders of positions of power and authority made it possible to generalize an economy of allocation, of which autochthonous peoples were not the only beneficiaries.

Tax exemptions, the obtaining of subsidized inputs, the extensive use of bank deficits, the guarantees provided by the state for foreign loans, the annulment of debts, preferential access to state contracts, and the trade in ivory, precious stones, and toxic wastes also constituted a source of profits for brokers and foreign business entrepreneurs who received various kinds of income. Generally speaking, this kind of political economy cared little for the imperatives of productivity. Internally, it led to an accelerated clientelism of the élites and intermediary bodies, citizenship becoming identical with receiving a salary. In addition, neither the local exploitation of the workforce nor the intensity of coercion sufficed decisively to increase the productivity of the economies and their competitiveness on the world stage.[75]

---

[75] Swedberg, "The Export Performance of Sub-Saharan Africa," *Economic Development and Cultural Change* 39 (1991): 540-566.

## Decompositions

The new situation involving international competition (relocation, the quest for advantages connected with low labor costs, the rise of industries in free-trade zones, business strategies of globalization, the volatility of the flow of capital) and the deregulation of trade that occurred in the 1980s forced these economies to reposition themselves within the world market.[76] Considering their nature, the forms of the integration with the outside and with specific forms of intervention on the part of foreign firms and local capital, it was not to be expected that this repositioning would take place in accord with the same modalities as those followed by certain countries in Southeast Asia—namely, by restructuring and reconverting industry in high technology sectors, diversifying service activities, increasing mastery of new forms of expertise, conquering new markets, levies on new flows of capital, and internationalizing production.[77]

In certain African countries, the general configuration of the market, the industrial base, the structure of relationships between the bureaucracy and local business milieus, and the nature of their respective connections with multinational companies, did not allow access to new technologies and new networks of distribution, the building-up of a substantial body of practical knowledge, or the encouragement of an entrepreneurial dynamism that could have helped these countries to respond in a creative

---

[76] On these developments, see P. Hirst and J. Zeitlin, "Flexible Specialization versus Post-Fordism: Theory, Evidence, and Policy Implications," *Economy and Society* 20 (1991): 1-56. See also G. R. D. Underhill, "Markets Beyond Politics? The State and the Internationalization of Financial Markets," *European Journal of Political Research* 19 (1991): 197-225.

[77] Cf. A. Amsden, "Third World Industrialization: 'Global Fordism' or a New Model?" *New Left Review* 182 (1990): 5-31.

way to the constraints of the world economy, as happened elsewhere.[78] Because these economies are exterior to the triad North America-Western Europe-Pacific Rim, and still more because their local structures of promotion were not very effective and because it was hardly possible to find in them the productive combinations sought by international capital, they could not take advantage of relocation to provide outlets for industries producing intermediary goods to allow investments directed toward high-technology products intended for export, or to specialize in international financial activities.

As a result, they could not participate in an active and profitable way in the new international division of labor. Hence it is understandable that the new wave of the internationalization of capital is able to ignore them, all the more because since the end of the Cold War, the opening of markets in the East and in the former Soviet Union, along with the continuing tyranny and disorder in Africa, have accentuated the decline in continent's role on both the economic and the ideological and symbolic levels. In addition to this inability to turn international factors to its advantage, we must also note the extraordinary pressure exerted by the compression, on a world-wide scale, of financial time, and its current reduction to a purely digital time. This transformation is not unconnected with the development of new technologies of communication and payment. The gap between the digital time of financial operations on the global scale and the historical time of real economic adjustments has steadily increased. The priority accorded speculative activities (one of the characteristics of globalization), abetted by the structural inertia of African economies, has had a deleterious

---

[78] See for example J. Chalmers, "Political Institutions and Economic Performances: The Government-Business Relationship in Japan, South Korea, and Taiwan," in F. Deyo, ed. *The Political Economy of the New Asian Industrialism* (Ithaca NY: Cornell University Press, 1987).

effect on productive activities. One result of this gap between differing scales of time and production is that whole sectors of African economies have gone underground.

To all these factors we should add the pressures resulting from the execution of plans for structural adjustment. The latter are of several kinds. Let us consider first the specifically economic effects. On this level, one must of course take into account the variety of cases. And, to be sure, one must take into consideration the differing application of these programs, depending on the countries involved, the discontinuities in their execution, the way in which the measures recommended by international lenders were diverted, rearranged, or corrupted by local bureaucracies, the structures of production in the countries that applied them, and the coalitions that supported or opposed them.[79] However, no matter what the variations, it remains that the results of these programs were far from conclusive, from a strictly economic point of view. Even in contexts where they were carried out in a more or less sustained and systematic way, the rise in exports turned out to be insufficient to ensure debt payments, despite the magnitude of the devaluations.[80]

On the whole, abandoning price controls has not had the intended jump-starting effects. The reduction of deficits has taken place at the price of a clear decrease in public investments and, in some cases, of ordinary operating expenses. Often the burdens of internal debt have remained,

---

[79] On some of these questions, see J. W. Thomas and M. S. Grindle, "After the Decision: Implementing Policy Reforms in Developing Countries," *World Development* 18 (1990): 1163-81; J. Nelson, ed., *Economic Crisis and Policy Choice: The Politics of Adjustment in the Third World* (Princeton: Princeton University Press, 1990).

[80] Cf. the case of Ghana as studied by D. Rothchild, ed., *Ghana: The Political Economy of Recovery* (Boulder CO: Lynne Rienner Publications, 1991).

while the decrease in state spending on salaries and the acceleration of price increases has had a depressive effect on consumer spending and private investment. In most African countries that were subjected to these programs, the gross domestic product fell. And although pressure grew, the fiscal crisis was accentuated even as the level of net transfers of capital abroad in the form of debt servicing (and various leaks) remained constant or, worse yet, increased. The sinking of whole sectors of the economy into parallel circuits went on at an unprecedented pace, the underground part of transactions and arrangements (including certain operations of privatization) having extended its ramifications into international trade.

The social and political effects were even more serious. We have seen how, from the point of view of the postcolonial African state, what passed for citizenship did not confer political rights as such, whether in the form of the right to individual representation, social rights, or the right to work. Between the state and the individual intervened the family, the lineage, the network of relatives, even religious brotherhoods. Did the individual find himself without resources and threatened even in his subsistence? It was not the state's role to ensure him the most elementary protection. His network of relatives took responsibility for him. Was he sinking into disinheritance, drifting, and poverty? He had no claim on the state, with which he had, particularly in this domain, no face-to-face relationship.

We have also seen how the private appropriation of public resources sometimes assumed the role of an integrating mechanism, the appropriated useful goods almost never being consumed for the exclusive benefit of a single individual, even if they were redistributed one by one, according to relationships of allegiance. Finally, we have seen how postcolonial African regimes tried to bring most of the population within disciplinary systems by using the mechanism of salaries, the latter

58

amounting, on close inspection, to favors allocated for the purpose of institutionalizing a form of domination that had its own basis in law.

Today, these systems as a whole are being shaken by two kinds of upheavals. On the one hand, there are the pressures put on African economies by financing and the structures of foreign trade. On the other hand, there is the horizon opened by a threefold process including (1) the appearance of new forms of political mobilization (which should not be confused with a transition toward democracy), (2) skimming, and then the decomposition of the state in the context of a resurgence of the predatory economy that characterized Africa in the nineteenth century, and (3) the apparent generalization of war and armed violence as the primary means of resolving conflicts. These upheavals are likely to widen the fractures within African societies, just as class conflict formerly widened those in Western societies.

However, no matter how enlightening it may be, the difference between African experience and that of the Western world remains important. We now know that in the West, the conflict regarding labor, production, and the appropriation of profit was not solely an economic conflict. It also had to do with a representation of the world, of society, and of political sovereignty. At stake was the development of a gigantic process of cultural reconstruction, on which depended the transition toward a market economy. This transition was achieved thanks to three factors. First, the conflict over labor, production, and the appropriation of profit opened the path to the institutionalization of social fractures, that is, to the legitimacy of transforming them into subjects of political and ideological debate. Second, this conflict constituted in itself a powerful vector of the socialization and integration of the masses. Third, insofar as the capitalist mode of growth allowed, this transition contributed to the Keynesian regulation of the economy by setting up a form of profit-sharing favorable to mass consumption and to the establishment of a kind of compromise state: the providential state.

Such transformations were possible only because, despite the violence of labor struggles, which themselves tended to bring workers together and to shape collective identities, salaried workers and employers shared what might be called a common material *imaginaire,* production itself being considered a social good. Thanks to mechanisms that institutionalized antagonisms on the basis of a representation of interests, thanks to the full exercise of suffrage, and as a result of the decline of the view that force was the only remedy for social problems, conflicts within society were calmed. It was in this way that revolutions carried out in the name of poverty were avoided.[81]

The African situation is following a different trajectory. The policies of deregulation put in place in the 1980s led to an increase of poverty among the masses, though these policies were not the only cause of this increase. At least up to that point, the neo-liberal way out of the crisis had not enabled economic growth to begin again.[82] The deepening of poverty is connected with several factors, one of the most important being the difficulty of holding onto a job.[83] In fact, in the course of the last fifteen years, throughout Africa the labor market has become highly stratified.

---

[81] Cf., among others, the studies by J. Donzelot, *L'invention du social* (Paris: Fayard, 1984); A. O. Hirschman, *Deux siècles de rhétorique réactionnaire* (Paris: Fayard, 1991); P. Rosanvallon, *Le sacre du citoyen* (Paris: Gallimard, 1994).

[82] On these aspects, see for example R. Kanbur, *La pauvreté et les dimensions sociales de l'ajustement structurel en Côte d'Ivoire*, (Washington DC: World Bank, working paper no. 2, 1990).

[83] Cf. J. P. Lachaud, ed., *Pauvreté et marché de travail urbain en Afrique subsaharienne: analyse comparative* (Geneva: Institut International d'études sociales, 1994).

To be sure, regular, protected, salaried work has not entirely disappeared. But the proportion of individuals who are doing it has continually decreased to the point that one can justifiably suggest that at the end of this century the African work force is becoming less and less salaried. Irregular work is increasingly common. For whole sectors of the population, monthly remuneration has been replaced by occasional payments. Declared and disguised unemployment and long-term—thus not situation-bound—exclusion from the labor market afflicts an increasing proportion of households. A multi-dimensional insecurity has developed: "forced inactivity, brutal declines in fired workers' standard of living, workers rehired at low wages as temporary contract employees, unemployed diploma-holders, an exacerbated competition in a labor market saturated with countless small-scale activities seeking customers who are just as short of cash and who often fail to pay their bills, the coming and going of precarious and temporary work, the high rate of school dropouts, the daily struggle to earn enough money to survive from day to day, rent to be paid, medicines to buy, school costs to be paid, the instrumentalization and hardening of social relationships under the pressure of scarcity..."[84]

By their casual treatment of the international factors determining African stagnation, neo-liberal policies of limitless deregulation are thus undermining the formulas through which postcolonial power had in practice succeeded, at least in some countries, in achieving more or less dynamic compromises with autochthonous systems of coercion and in financing relationships of subjection. When we add the long-term developments secretly working on African societies (the demographic transitions taking place in rural regions and the intensification of migrations, the deterioration of the environment and the crisis in nomadic

---

[84] A. Marie, "'Y a pas l'argent'...," 304-05.

life, the drastic decline of revenues derived from plantation agriculture, the entropy of local systems of production and the redefinition of village powers, the emergence of urban power with its culture of riots and racketeering, the accentuated saturation of the real estate market and the intense competition for land in certain regions of the continent, the rarefaction of jobs in the so-called modern sector of the economy, the impoverishment of the salaried classes and whole sectors of the economy going underground, new ways of securing and exploiting labor, the formation of refugee movements and the use of prisoners of war as mercenaries, the increasing criminalization of the ruling classes and the militarization of commerce), we realize that these policies directly affect postcolonial African regimes on two levels: first, the material and social bases on which they have been based up to now and the *imaginaires* that supported them, and second, the way in which they legitimated themselves.[85]

In reality, the brutal deflation of the public and parapublic sectors brought about the dissolution of a great number of state companies. Subjected to serious decreases in personnel, substantial reductions in salaries, or simply large-scale layoffs, the privatization of public enterprises and the slimming-down of public functions contributed to the blockage of

---

[85] On these long-term developments, see for example C. Faussey-Domalain and P. Vinard, "Agriculture de rente and démographie dans le Sud-est ivoirien. Une économie villageoise assistée en milieu forestier péri-urbain," *Revue Tiers Monde* 32 (1991): 03-114; the studies collected in "État et sociétés nomades," *Politique africaine* 34 (1989); S. Reyna, ed., *Land and Society in Contemporary Africa* (Hanover NH: University Press of New England, 1988); A. Zolberg et al., "International Factors in the Formation of Refugee Movements," *International Migration Review* 20 (1986): 151-169; M. F. Jarret and F. R. Mahieu, "Ajustement structurel, croissance et répartition: l'exemple de la Côte d'Ivoire," *Revue Tiers Monde* 32 (1991): 39-62.

the system of inter-communitarian transfers, thereby reactivating conflicts concerning the distribution of wealth and once again raising the question of the very morality of the system of inequality and domination forged after independence, as is shown by the rise in the number of accusations of sorcery, the constantly increasing success of Pentecostal religious discourses, the reestablishment of militant Islam around the perimeter of the Sahel and the Indian Ocean, the proliferation of therapeutic itineraries and methods of healing, the emergence of new languages of protest and the rise of rural robbery and urban criminality.[86]

At the same time, the collapse of export income and the restructuring of the offices concerned with commercializing cash products has extended insolvency to planters, industrials, and bankers, bringing to a halt all the activities that depended on public markets and indirectly supplied the labyrinth of parallel economic circuits.[87] This has affected the very armature of these formulas of domination, since the system of subsistence incomes and gifts on which their legitimacy was partly based has been corrupted, and in most cases no longer has at its disposal the means to reproduce itself. But contrary to the expectations of international lenders, the drying up of subsistence incomes, as a result of deadlines set by structural adjustment programs, may well lead not only to a prolonged decline of the state, but also to an extraordinary fragmentation of the market, the two processes promoting, more than one might expect, an uncontrolled wave of violence. Consequently, the programs of structural

---

[86] On some of these events, see P. Geschiere, *Sorcellerie et politique en Afrique* (Paris: Karthala, 1995).
[87] See H. L. van der Laan and W. T. M. van Haaren, "African Marketing Boards Under Structural Adjustment: The Experience of Sub-Saharan Africa during the 1980s" (Leiden: Afrika StudieCentrum, Working Paper no. 13, 1993) and P. Hugon, "L'impact des politiques d'ajustement structurels sur les circuits financiers informels africains," *Revue Tiers Monde* 31 (1990): 325-49.

adjustment have an interest, not from the point of view of their aptitude for reconnecting Africa to the world economy, but also from the point of view of the perverse effects they produce and the way in which the latter erode the postcolonial compromise mentioned above, by emasculating the traditional instruments of state power and bring about, a profound modification of social structures and cultural attitudes.

At the end of the twentieth century, among the options open to Africa, two are of particular interest to us here. The first is the option of looking forward to the coming century and successfully responding to the challenge of productivity, that is, of turning to Africa's advantage the conditions of its relationship to the external market.[88] The second is a "return" to the nineteenth century. The conflict with the global market will not be decided to the advantage of the continent if it continues to be negotiated within the framework of programs of structural adjustment. Essentially, these programs propose only a return to the 1960s, when the structure of African economies made them chiefly net exporters of tropical products.

But with or without international lenders, Africa must confront the challenge of the competitiveness of its economies on the global scale. This challenge cannot be victoriously met in the current configuration of the world economy, that is, ultimately, without the establishment of intensive ways of constructing inequality and organizing social exclusion. But we have seen that during the colonial period, the relationships among violence, the production of inequality, and the accumulation of wealth were of an extraordinary complexity. There are not necessarily any causal connections among these three variables. The

---

[88] On the complexity of such a leap forward, see A. Amsden, *Asia's Next Giant: South Korea and Late Industrialization* (New York: Oxford University Press, 1989).

transition to democracy will depend on the way in which debate on the legitimacy of social exclusion is resolved historically (and to the advantage of which social forces); otherwise, how would it be possible to legitimate and codify it institutionally? Here we see the complexity of this kind of project, particularly in contexts in which redistribution has long constituted the social and political mediation par excellence; and in which, more than ever, the problems of poverty and scarcity reignite social struggles, and on a larger scale than in the past.

# Part Two

# The Price of Force

The various questions raised in the course of the first part of this study must be approached by placing at the center of our analysis the three major historical events represented by the eviction of Africa from the regular world markets, the particular forms of its integration into the circuits of the international parallel economy, and the fragmentation of public power that accompanies these two processes. Moreover, through apparently unprecedented forms of insertion into the international system and the modes of economic exploitation that are their corollary, equally unprecedented forms of domination are taking shape, almost everywhere on the continent.

The crystallization of these new forms of domination will depend on how the victorious participants in the current struggles answer the following questions: Who is who? Who should be protected, by whom, against what, against whom, and at what price? Who is the equal of whom? To what do I have a right, by the sole fact of my membership of an ethnic group, a region, a religion, or a brotherhood? Who can take power and lead a country, under what circumstances, how, for how long, and on what conditions? Who has a right to the product of whose labor and in exchange for what compensations? When can one cease to obey authority without being punished? Who should punish whom and for what reasons? Who should pay taxes and what are taxes for? Who can contract debts in the name of whom, to whom should loans be granted and who should repay them? To whom does a country's wealth belong?

All these questions have to do with the very pillars of the social order, without which there is no social order at all. The political economies put into operation since the beginning of the 1980s, military activity, elections, and more generally, what are often called, somewhat hastily, "transitions toward democracy," are some of the attempts to respond to these fundamental questions.[89] But political liberalization—which, moreover, may be accompanied by the persistence of authoritarianism and the decline of the state—is only one aspect, and perhaps not the most decisive one, of the current mutations. Because the formulas of domination to which we refer and new procedures for the formation of private property are still being constituted, they have not yet, generally speaking, supplanted those that preceded them. Sometimes they are inspired by them, retain traces of them, or even function under their mask.

The observation made above entails another central idea: the issue of African societies' ability to govern themselves—that is, to establish a creative equilibrium between the use of violence and the constitution of a system of private property—is played out at the interstices of two processes. The first of these processes threatens to produce an internal dissolution under the cumulative impact of what might be called global pressure (particularly debt and the conditions connected with its repayment) and internal pressure (particularly the still uncodified struggles concerning the relationship among identity, inequality, and access to rare resources). The second process has to do with the risks of a generalized loss of control over violence, both public and private. This uncontrolled violence is set in motion, on the one hand, by the aggravation of inequalities and corruption, and on the other, by the persistence of fundamental disagreements regarding the way to conduct the battles currently

---

[89] The literature on "transitions" toward democracy is abundant, if often not convincing. See the brief synthesis by M. Diouf, "Libéralisations politiques et transitions démocratiques: perspectives africaines," a paper presented at the eighth General Assembly of the CODESRIA, Dakar, 26 June-2 July 1995. Or again, C. Monga, *Anthropology of Anger: Civil Society and Democracy in Africa* (Boulder CO: Lynne Rienner, 1996), chap. 1.

being waged (who is going to dominate and with what means). In Africa, the result of these deep movements may be the definitive defeat of the state as we have recently known it. However, they could just as well lead to a deepening of the state's indigenous character, or, more radically still, to the state's replacement, here and there, by mechanisms that will retain the name but whose intrinsic quality, attributes, and modes of operation will have nothing in common with those of the classical state.

## Short Time and Long Developments

Since the asymmetry of African countries' economic performances is becoming increasingly structural in nature, the effect of the continent's eviction from regular world markets varies in intensity, according to the country, region, product, or productive good concerned. The impact of external pressure on these countries' economies depends on whether or not they have put into operation serious policies of adjustment. The failure of processes of adjustment is not everywhere the same, or in any case, it does not produce the same effects everywhere. Moreover, there is no reason to suppose that this eviction itself is irreversible. On another level, African countries' insertion into circuits of the parallel international economy has not been halted by the efforts to liberalize import procedures. It is not clear that for the participants involved in these developments, the desire to avoid port taxes is alone sufficient to explain this phenomenon, which is not peculiar to the continent. In reality, it also affects, in more or less different forms, other regions of the world (South America, the territories of the former Soviet Union, and even several parts of Asia), where it contributes to changing the modes of the formation and distribution of revenues, the forms of sociability, the structures of the representation and mediation of economic and political interests, the conditions of appropriating the resources necessary for the sustenance of the dominant social relationships (in the case of taxes and other debits), questions relating to citizenship, and even the nature of the state.[90]

In Africa the current and foreseeable consequences of these events are of a different order and have a very special intensity. This development is spreading at a time when, the Cold War having ceased to structure power relationships on the global level and Africa having lost status on the international level, the continent is in the process of carrying out a genuine turnaround on itself—a turnaround to which the overworked concept of "crisis" is unfortunately not adequate. This turnaround is taking place on a scale of magnitude similar to the one which characterized similar processes in the middle of the nineteenth century, at the time when the slave trade was giving way to a so-called legitimate economy—processes that ended up in conquest and colonial occupation.[91]

---

[90] Cf. the studies collected in *Revue Tiers Monde* 33 (1992), especially G. Fonseca, "Economie de la drogue: taille, caractéristiques et impact économique"; B. Destremau, "Les enjeux du qat au Yémen"; and A. Labrousse, "La culture du pavot dans le district du Dir (Pakistan): Économie paysanne, productions illicites et alternatives de développement dans le contexte d'un conflit régionale."

[91] On this period, and for a political interpretation of these processes, see the overview by J. Lonsdale, "The European Scramble and Conquest in African History," in *The Cambridge History of Africa*, vol. 6 (Cambridge: Cambridge University Press, 1985): 680-766; B. O. Oloruntimehin, "The Impact of the Abolition Movement on the Social and Political Development of West Africa in the Nineteenth and Twentieth Centuries," *Ibadan* 7 (1972): 33-58. For an evaluation of the economic dimensions of this turning point, see, for example, A. G. Hopkins, *An Economic History of West Africa* (London: Longman, 1973); R. Law, ed., *From Slave Trade to "Legitimate" Commerce: The Commercial Transition in Nineteenth-Century West Africa* (Cambridge: Cambridge University Press, 1995).

To be sure, we must take into account the varying impact of these processes, depending on the regions, the rates of change, and the local temporalities (on the coast, in the hinterland, the intermediate countries, in societies with and without state formations).[92]  For the most part, however, the structural adjustment represented by the transition from an economy based on trade in slaves and ivory to one based on trade in cash crops (peanuts, palm oil, rubber, etc.) led to a transformation of the material foundations of these states.  The ways in which these states augmented their assets, increased the number of useful goods, and distributed the product of labor also changed.[93]  Moreover, territorial dilation, contraction, and retraction had always been a constitutive aspect of state-formation in Africa.[94]  As early as the seventeenth century, this development was already affecting several polities situated on the Atlantic coast and even farther into the interior.  A tradition of predatory states living on raiding, plundering, and the sale of captives had grown stronger.  On the basis of territorial fragmentation and the stagnation of structures, slave-trading military regimes, relieved of all civil responsibility, had been set up and endowed with the means, not necessarily of conquering territories and extending their sovereignty, but at least of appropriating their resources, both human and material.[95]  Other states, just as brutal as the former,

---

[92]  See on this subject F. Cooper, "Africa and the World Economy," *African Studies Review* 29 (1981).

[93]  See P. Manning, "Slaves, Palm Oil, and Political Power on the West African Coast," *African Historical Studies* 2 (1969): 279-88.

[94]  Cf. J. Lonsdale, "States and Social Processes in Africa," *African Studies Review* 29 (1981).

[95]  Useful information on the organization and functioning of these systems and the way in which political competition took place in them is to be found in C. Meillassoux, *Anthropologie de l'esclavage: le ventre de fer et d'argent* (Paris: Presses Universitaires de France, 1986), 143-235.

adopted a policy of assimilation toward their captives. Instead of using them as human merchandise, they obliged their captives to serve or work for them, or else forced the conquered peoples to pay heavy indemnities and countless levies.[96] On the Slave Coast in particular (Allada and Whydah), constant disorder had led to a prolonged collapse and then a dissolution of royal authority. Local chiefs took advantage of this to establish their independence. But rivalries within the élite flared up, and these state formations went down in the civil wars that ended up destroying what was left of political order.[97]

Alongside these processes of dislocation, there took place movements aiming at the reconstruction and relegitimation of authority. For example, at the beginning of the eighteenth century, Dahomey conquered its neighbors, who were riven by internal dissensions. But if war could serve as a means of conquering and occupying territories that had usually been subjected only to periodic raids, the use of violence did not necessarily resolve, by itself, the problem of stabilizing the political order and government as such. Thus, having taken power after the death of Agaja at the end of the violent battles of succession and a challenge to the monarchy on the part of priestly power, Tegbesu tried to reunify the élite by adopting, in the 1740s, a policy of terror, purges, and compromise. The combination of these three levers of domination allowed him, on the one hand, to physically eliminate his most intractable enemies and, on the other, to

---

[96] See the examples reported in E. Terray, *Une histoire du royaume abron du Gyaman* (Paris: Karthala, 1995), 189-90.

[97] See, in addition, S. Johnson, *The History of the Yoruba From the Earliest Times to the Beginning of the British Protectorate* (London, 1921), 206-273; S. A. Akintoye, *Revolution and Power Politics in Yorubaland, 1840-1893: Ibadan Expansion and the Rise of Ekitiparapo* (New York: Humanities Press, 1971).

intervene in factional battles at the local level by supporting those who accepted his authority. At the same time, he showered gifts and benefits on local chiefs and influential families. Then, by a judicious manipulation of dynastic and family networks, by shaping a royal cult and staging it in spectacular form (human sacrifices), and by redefining the attributes of royalty beneath a mask of continuity (the redistribution of wealth and privileges, the renovation of the juridical order), he began an effort to relegitimate power. The objective of this effort was to convert brute violence into authority.[98]

In the regions under Muslim influence in the interior, more or less similar transformations took place. Before the second half of the nineteenth century, the empires situated on the edge of the desert had established zones of raiding and capture to the south and east of the Lake Chad basin. Wars of capture and slavery did not have the sole result of making possible the constitution of military apparatuses and the management of resources and populations within the framework of a predatory economy. Though these two forms of violence involved destruction, depredation, and robbery, they also favored, at least in some cases, the emergence of centralized powers. In any case, they were the origin of

---

[98] On the political history of ancient Dahomey, cf. I. A. Akinjogbin, *Dahomey and Its Neighbours, 1708-1818* (Cambridge: Cambridge University Press, 1967). On the shaping of the royal cult through the practice of human sacrifice, see R. Law, "Human Sacrifice in Pre-Colonial West Africa," *African Affairs* 84 (1985): 53-87. Useful information regarding the redistribution of useful goods and privileges is found in C. Coquery-Vidrovitch, "La fête des coutumes au Dahomey," *Annales* 19 (1964): 696-716; K. Polanyi, *Dahomey and the Slave Trade* (Seattle: University of Washington Press, 1966). In addition, see R. Law, "Ideologies of Royal Power: The Dissolution and Reconstruction of Political Authority on the Slave Coast, 1680-1750," *Africa* 57 (1987): 321-44.

modes of political organization and very specific forms of social and symbolic reconstruction.

The same was true for relationships among sovereignty, territoriality, and citizenship. Contrary to premature and superficial claims, the idea that political power and sovereignty are exercised through the mediation of the soil was not unknown in these regions.[99] However, territory was neither the sole support of political communities, nor the sole mark of sovereignty, nor the sole basis for civil obedience. Representations and uses of space were multiple, especially when they were intimately connected with the definition of the principles of membership and exclusion.[100] In a context in which captive-taking raids were common, the establishment of political spaces and areas of sovereignty could be achieved by imposing tributes on subject peoples, whose lives might be spared, for example. Citizenship itself could depend upon the mode of protection one enjoyed against the possibility of capture and sale. Family relationships as such might be replaced or supplemented by other forms of relationship (dependents, slaves, clients, hostages) that made possible other modalities of legitimate exploitation. A mixing of political, cultural, and religious identities was occurring on an unprecedented scale. The Baghirmi, for instance, borrowed his models of military and family organization and his titles from Kanem-Bornu. Elements of Islamic culture (clothes, systems of divination, etc.) spread among non-Muslims. Within these truly transnational and multicultural societies, religious networks and commercial exchanges were interlaced. And pressure or

---

[99] C. C. Stewart, "Frontier Disputes and Problems of Legitimation: Sokoto-Macina Relations, 1817-1837," *Journal of African History* 17 (1976):495-514.

[100] This is demonstrated very well by E. Terray, *Une histoire du royaume abron du Gyaman: Des origines à la conquête coloniale* (Paris: Karthala, 1995).

belonging to a territory almost never put an end to the multiplicity of allegiances and the plurality of loyalties.

During the second half of the nineteenth century, however, the Muslim frontier shifted, and vast regions of the northern part of Central Africa were caught between the advance from the Nile river valley and the advance from the west. Slavery as a relationship of subjection and the chief modality of extorting property and useful goods was greatly intensified, at the same time as the quest for ivory. Conquests, migrations, and other movements of populations fleeing marauders, mercenaries, and slave-traders led to the transformation of the customary models of social organization, registers of political action, and forms of exchange. The model of domination (half-suzerain, half-sultan) that resulted from these disturbances attained its point of absolute maximization with the Khartoumites.[101] With the support of the jallaba (itinerant brokers whose activity in the region predated the arrival of the Egyptians), they militarized commerce and specialized in slave-taking raids and ivory-trading. Proceeding by military force, political alliances, the incorporation of slaves and a judicious redistribution of tributes and long-distance commercial products, they set up the system of zariba (a group of small, fortified commercial colonies). When it proved necessary to do so, they made pacts with the indigenous peoples and thus set up strong

---

[101] As D. Cordell reminds us, the history of the Khartoumites is closely linked to Egyptian expansion into what is now Sudan and into northwest Zaïre. Between 1821 and 1879, in fact, Muhammad Ali and his successors had arrogated a virtual empire at the heart of Africa. The Egyptians had established themselves in Khartoum, and with the support of merchants of various nationalities, they had infiltrated their own agents throughout the region. These agents had joined forces with the itinerant merchants who were already there. See D. Cordell, "The Savanna Belt of North-Central Africa," in D. Birmingham and P. M. Martin, eds., History of Central Africa (London: Longman, 1990), 1: 64-65.

networks that dominated the whole of these territories up to the time of the Mahdist rebellion.[102]

Along the Atlantic coast as in the interior, a large number of independent political entities disintegrated under the weight of external debt and internal tyranny. In the course of the nineteenth century, these dislocations had led to significant cultural reconstructions clearly marked by the massive conversions to monotheistic religions,[103] acute crises of sorcery,[104] the appearance of numerous healing movements, the transformation of refugee communities into hordes of mercenaries, and a certain number of uprisings that were often carried out in the name of Islam.[105] The collapse of the demand for slaves had not led to a diminution of tensions. On the contrary, peoples and ethnic groups who had succeeded in maintaining their brokering privileges and in establishing their domination over the great commercial crossroads increased their demographic expansion and

---

[102] See D. Cordell, "The Savanna Belt...," 30-74. Regarding developments on the south Atlantic coast, see, in the same collection, the study by J. C. Miller, "The Paradoxes of Impoverishment in the Atlantic Zone," 118-159.

[103] Cf. J. F. A. Ajayi, *Christian Missions in Nigeria, 1841-1891: The Making of a New Élite* (Evanston IL: Northwestern University Press, 1969), 1-24; J. and J. Comaroff, *Of Revelation and Revolution: Christianity, Colonialism, and Consciousness in South Africa*, vol. 1 (Chicago: University of Chicago Press, 1991).

[104] A. J. H. Latham, *Witchcraft Accusations and Economic Tension in Pre-Colonial Old Calabar," Journal of African History* 13 (1972): 249-260.

[105] M. Last, "Reform in West Africa: The Jihad Movements of the Nineteenth Century," in J. F. A. Ajayi and M. Crowder, eds., *History of West Africa*, vol. 2 (London: Longman, 1988); M. Klein, "Social and Economic Factors in the Muslim Revolution in Senegambia," *Journal of African History* 14 (1972): 419-441.

procured rifles, thus endowing themselves with new means of acquiring property.[106]

Under the leadership of the heads of slave-trading gangs, armed groups, and merchant-adventurers[107] (El-Zubeir Pasha, Rabeh and the black sultans of Ubangi, the Afro-Arabic Tippu Tipp, Msiri of Katanga, Mirambo and his commercial empire in northern Tabora), predatory movements had emerged.[108] They reactivated caravan commerce and, through raiding, the authoritarian system of tribute, the recruitment of thousands of porters, and the local reintroduction of slavery, they aggravated the disturbance of customary structures, clouded ancestral charters, and caused significant displacements of populations.[109] These new operators (traffickers, brokers, gang-leaders, marabout groups, businessmen of various kinds) set out to shape to their own advantage the economic conversion that was going on. Using war as an instrument, they established more or less informal systems

---

[106] Cf. J. E. Inikori, "The Import of Firearms into West Africa, 1750-1807: A Quantitative Analysis," *Journal of African History* 18 (1977): 339-368; B. Awe, "Militarism and Economic Development in Nineteenth-Century Yoruba Country: The Ibadan Example," *Journal of African History* 14 (1973): 65-78.

[107] See for example El-Zubeir Pasha, *Black Ivory, or the Story of El-Zubeir Pasha, Slaver and Sultan, as Told by Himself,* trans. H. C. Jackson (New York, 1970); W. K. R. Hallam, "The Itinerary of Rabih Fadl Allah, 1879-1893," *Bulletin de l'Institut Fondamental de l'Afrique Noire* 30, series B (1968): 165-81, as well as his biography of Rabeh, *The Life and Times of Rabih Fadl Allah* (London, 1977); R. A. Adeleye, "Rabih b. Fadallah, 1879-93: Exploits and Impact on Political Relations in Central Sudan," *Journal of the Historical Society of Nigeria* 2 (1970): 223-42.

[108] See for example M. F. Page, "The Manyema Hordes of Tippu Tipp," *International Journal of African Historical Studies* 1 (1974): 69-84.

[109] See for example S. P. Reyna, *Wars Without End: The Political Economy of a Precolonial African State* (Hanover NH, University Press of New England, 1990).

of taxation and took control of the main regional crossroads and commercial networks. Having virtually extra-territorial rights and proceeding by raiding, taking booty, and practicing tribute, they completed the criminalization of economic activity and of the very act of governing. After the slave-trading bloodbath, Africa's reentry into the international economic system took place by way of an extortion of its raw materials. Toward the end of the nineteenth century, this system of violence and brutality was prolonged through concessionary systems.[110] Vast enterprises with commercial and mining privileges and sovereign rights authorizing them to levy taxes and maintain armed forces, intensified the process of depredation and the breakup of lineages and clans, and institutionalized a regime based on murder. Under the protection of the colonial bureaucratic apparatus, the market had begun to function in a gangster-like way.

The developments briefly described above led to three decisive consequences. On the one hand, the increasing debts accumulated by local princes and commercial élites led, almost everywhere, to the decline of African polities' external power, exposing them to serious threats of internal collapse.[111] On the other hand, although it did not reach the levels that characterized the period of the slave trade, the degree of violence and depredation required by the new modes of entry into the international economy promoted not only the militarization of power and commerce and the intensification of extortion, but also the destruction of the

---

[110] Cf. C. Coquery-Vidrovitch's classic study, *Le Congo au temps des grandes compagnies concessionnaires, 1898-1930* (Paris: Mouton, 1977).

[111] The cycle of going into debt was not new. Moreover, it had been one of the main cornerstones of the slave trade, as is shown by J. Miller's study, *Way of Death* (Madison: University of Wisconsin Press, 1988). See also H. Gemery and J. Hogendorn, eds., *The Uncommon Market: Essays in the Economic History of the Atlantic Slave Trade* (New York, 1978), 303-30.

balances that had formerly governed the relationships between holding public power and pursuing private gain.[112] The rush to trade in ivory and rubber, the trading-post economy, and the concessionary economy completed the destabilization of these balances between 1850 and 1930.[113] Finally, there were substantial transformations in the way people conceived the relationships between their membership in a political community and the channels of access to property that this membership opened or did not open. Religious and identity-shaping systems, the procedures of legitimating authority, the social and political construction of rights, duties, transfers, and obligations, even the norms that governed the rules of civility and contracts, commercial morality and civic virtue: all these were redefined.[114]

From these remarks, it should not be concluded that Africa is in the process of moving backward, and that everything that is happening there today is only a repetition of a scenario and a historical phase that people wrongly thought it had moved beyond. While borrowing some of their characteristics from

---

[112] Cf. B. Barry, *La Sénégambie* (Paris: L'Harmattan, 1986); I. Wilks, *Asante in the Nineteenth Century* (Cambridge: Cambridge University Press, 1975); R. Richards, "Production and Reproduction in Warrior States: Segu Bambara and Segu Tokolor, c. 1712-1890," *International Journal of African Historical Studies* 13 (1980): 389-419; R. Law, "Royal Monopoly and Private Enterprise in the Atlantic Trade: The Case of Dahomey," *Journal of African History* 18 (1977): 555-77.

[113] C. Coquery-Vidrovitch, *Le Congo au temps des compagnies concessionnaires 1898-1930* (Paris: Mouton, 1972); R. Harms. "The End of Red Rubber: A Reassessment," *Journal of African History* 16 (1975): 73-88.

[114] I. Wilks, *Asante in the Nineteenth Century* (Cambridge: Cambridge University Press, 1975); G. I. Jones, *The Trading States of the Oil Rivers* (London: Oxford University Press, 1963); J. M. Janzen, *Lemba 1650-1930: A Drum of Affliction in Africa and the New World* (New York: Garland, 1982); S. Feierman, *Peasant Intellectuals* (Madison: University of Wisconsin Press, 1988).

late nineteenth-century models of stagnation, the new ways of disemboweling the continent cannot be reduced to them, for several reasons. First, and in contrast with the nineteenth century, the current is currently flowing in the opposite direction, that is, from the regular and formal international economy towards obscure channels whose branches, although invisible, are nonetheless international (trafficking in drugs and armaments, illicit movements of money).[115] This outlet is neither a pure and simple disconnection[116] nor a "disengagement" as such, nor yet a marginalization in the strict sense of the word. It is one of the facets of a more complex development that is taking place on a worldwide scale. It represents the other side of a "world time" in which a changing multiplicity of temporalities intermesh.[117] Several different processes coexist in this meshing of temporalities: processes of homogenizing images at the same time as processes of producing differences and heterogeneities.[118] In short, contradictory dynamics overlap, composed of gaps, disjunctions, and different rhythms, which we cannot reduce to a simple antagonism between internal and external forces. More decisively, current developments— we have seen that their central feature is the mobilization of violence with the goal of amassing property—are combining, and making up a system

---

[115] This "global character" is not new. It has its own history. See P. Curtin, *Cross-Cultural Trade in World History* (Cambridge: Cambridge University Press, 1984); F. Braudel, *Civilization and Capitalism, 15th-18th Centuries*, 3 vols. (London: Collins, 1981-84).

[116] D. Bach speaks of "déconnexion par défaut" in "Europe-Afrique: des acteurs en quête de scénarios," *Études internationales* 22 (1991): 336.

[117] Cf. the analysis offered in A. Appadurai, "Disjuncture and Difference in the Global Cultural Economy," *Public Culture* 2 (1990): 1-24.

[118] On this subject, see J. F. Bayart, ed., *La réinvention du capitalisme* (Paris: Karthala, 1994), esp. 9-43.

in such an unusual way that the result is not only debt, the destruction of productive capital, and war, but also the deflation of the state, and, in certain cases, its decline and a radical questioning of it as a public benefit, a general technology of domination, and a privileged instrument for ensuring the protection and security of individuals and for creating the juridical conditions under which political rights can be extended and the exercise of citizenship is made possible.

## Systems of Property and Systems of Sovereignty

The peculiarity of this development is clear if we consider the unintended but quite real effects of policies of structural adjustment and of the dynamics of conditionality (conditions of an economic order attached to loans granted to African countries by international financial institutions in the course of the past ten years). First of all, it has not been sufficiently emphasized in this regard that one of the major political events of the end of this century is the crumbling of African states' independence and sovereignty, and their (surreptitious) subjection to the supervision of international lenders. Relatively speaking, this situation recalls the one that affected Egypt and Tunisia in the 1870s when, in order to repay their debts, these countries had imposed upon them consular regimes and, against the background of the dissolution of political authority, were deprived of an important number of the attributes of their sovereignty, particularly in the financial and fiscal domains. Toward the end of the 1980s, African countries began to follow a more or less similar path. The decline of their external power had placed, de facto, many states in a system that might be called "fragmented sovereignty." The government by proxy exercised by the World Bank, the International Monetary Fund, and lenders (whether public or private) is no longer limited to requiring respect for great principles and macroeconomic balances. In practice, supervision by international lenders has been considerably strengthened

83

and is henceforth manifested by a range of direct interventions in internal economic management, including credit control, the execution of privatizations, the definition of consumer needs, import policies, agricultural programs, the reduction of costs, and direct control of the treasury.[119]

This situation—which could, however, not be compared to a process of recolonization pure and simple—is not peculiarly African, since countries throughout the world have been (and are still) subjected to the same steam roller.[120] Two main consequences nonetheless give the African case a special form. On the one hand, because of the brutality of the payments it requires, the redeployment of constraints, and the new forms of subjection it imposes on the most needy and vulnerable sectors of the population, this kind of government by proxy brings together in a single dynamic elements belonging to the register of what is imposed on countries defeated in war and to the register of the conduct of a civil policy. At the heart of this new dispensation, the logic of the emasculation of the state goes hand in hand with the logic of the excision of sovereignty. To understand the way the logic of sovereignty made possible strategies of amassing property that were less violent than current ones, perhaps it would be useful to recall that during the 1980s, the leading explanation for the "African crisis" consisted in putting the responsibility on the state and on the excessive levies it imposed—so people thought—on the economy. The restoration of the state's legitimacy and the way out of the crisis depended, it was said, on the

---

[119] See J. Coussy, "État minimum et dépolitisation sous la pression des contraintes extérieures: le cas des pays en développement," doc. pol, Paris, 1992.

[120] S. Haggard and R. Kaufman, eds., *The Politics of Adjustment: International Constraints, Distributive Conflicts, and the State* (Princeton: Princeton University Press, 1992).

state's ability to avoid the pressure of social demands (the organization of public services, health, education, the allocation of resources and revenues, redistributions of all kinds) and to let market forces work autonomously, within a field that would henceforth be free.[121] In doing so, it was supposed that the transition to a market economy would require bracketing individual political and citizenship rights, that is, suspending the rights and debts that allow individuals to have not only duties and obligations toward the state but also claims on it—claims that can be asserted politically, for example by demanding public services. The result of the insistence on dismantling all state interventions in the economy (whether these take the form of controls, subsidies, or protections) without at the same time making the state itself more effective, and without assigning to it, in a positive manner, new functions, has been to undermine the material bases (already very fragile), to disrupt (without restructuring them positively) the logics of the constitution of clienteles and coalitions, and to diminish the state's ability to sustain itself. All this has opened the way to the state's decline.

Secondly, the controls, subsidies, and protections whose dismantling is now required were not limited to the fiscal and administrative dimension. They were not simply distributive in nature, and indeed in certain cases they were productive. They also made possible a set of conceptions of legitimate political activity and of forms of social violence that were accepted because they were highly regulated. All this taken together

---

[121] Cf. the discussion carried on by T. M. Callaghy on the subject of the desirable balance between the logic of the market and the logic of the state, and the necessity of "protecting" the élites in charge of conceiving and carrying out economic reforms against purely political logics, in "Vision and Politics in the Transformation of the Global Political Economy: Lessons from the Second and Third Worlds," University of Pennsylvania, Philadelphia, October 1991, pp. 8-12.

85

made possible a certain social and political cohesion, an order of domination based on coercion, to be sure, but also on exchanges, transfers, reciprocity, and obligations.[122] In the countries of "useful Africa," it was this form of government that prevented, in most cases, a drift into pure and simple arbitrariness and summary violence.

The same factors also ended up providing a minimum social basis for some of these regimes. In this context, they could demand submission and obedience on the part of their subjects in exchange for a generalized distribution of salaried positions. As we have shown elsewhere, the state used salaries to buy the population's obedience and to subject it to disciplinary apparatuses. In most cases, salaries were what legitimated subjection. An essential part of the constitution of a kind of citizenship that was not primarily founded on the principle of political equality and representation, it "was based on the existence of obligations through which the state made claims on society," the construction of the relationship of subjection being carried out in the distributive order and not in that of the equivalence of human beings endowed with natural and civil rights of their own. By transforming salary into an obligation, the state granted subsistence incomes to its debtors. These subsistence incomes "did not sanction a process of converting energy into wealth. They outlined a particular figure of obedience and domination."[123] Moreover, in certain countries these obligations were considered, if not as favors, at least as privileges. Thus one can assert that the salaried individual, the citizen, and the client mutually supported each other, or in any case participated in a single structure of conscious representations that clearly denotes what

---

[122] F. R. Mahieu, "Principes économiques et société africaine," *Tiers Monde* 30 (1989): 725-753.

[123] See A. Mbembe and J. Roitman, "Figures of the Subject in Times of Crisis," *Public Culture* 16 (1995).

has been called "the politics of the stomach."[124]   It is this formula of domination, that is, of controlling people and the allocation of goods, profits, and percentages that is threatened by austerity, the weight of external constraint, and war.  Because of generalized insolvency and material devastation, almost everywhere in Africa the state has been put in a position where it is incapable of carrying out the necessary arbitrations and defining the social compromises that are indispensable not only for any consistent transition to a market economy as it is envisaged by international financial institutions, but also for the production of public order itself.

Thirdly, it is not only that by shifting the site of political, regulatory, and technical choices, the very sources of power have been transferred to international supervisors at the same time that certain attributes of sovereignty have been erased.  There has also been a shift in the sources of legitimacy and influence, and this has resulted in a blurring of the criteria of accountability, since those who impose policies are not only invisible to the populations affected, but also different from those who are directly responsible for their consequences in the eyes of their people.  Those who should be responsible to the people for these policies act as if by proxy, and not on the basis of the sovereign capacity that is supposed to characterize the state.  Financial strangling and fiscal crisis have promoted the multiplication of conflicts concerning the redistribution of subsistence incomes and gifts (the allocation of bank credits, the granting of government contracts, the attribution of what remains of privileges, advantages, and bonuses, the assignment of equipment and infrastructures, the ethno-regional distribution of import-export licenses, grants, credits, jobs, and favors), producing an abundance of highly

---

[124] J. F. Bayart, *L'État en Afrique: La politique du ventre* (Paris: Fayard, 1989). See also P. Geschiere, *Sorcellerie et politique en Afrique* (Paris: Karthala, 1995).

contradictory conceptions of what a political community ought to be and of the connection between different kinds of citizenship within a single political space (ethnicity and nation, autochthonous and allogenic individuals) on the one hand, and the range of resources on which the right of possession can be exercised, on the other.

The state has lost much of the ability to regulate and arbitrate that allowed it to construct its legitimacy. As a result, it no longer has at its disposal the financial resources of administrative power, and in general, all the other kinds of goods that would have made possible a political resolution of the countless conflicts that now lead, almost everywhere, to violent actions, which had previously been contained within more or less tolerable limits. Without entitlements to hand out or to honor, and without anything much to distribute, the state no longer has any public credibility. When it arrives at this point, the state has only the instrument of violence—on which, however, it no longer holds a monopoly. The regulation of violence on the internal level, in a context marked by material devastation, disorganization, the reconstruction of the circuits of credit and production, and a brutal decline of notions of the public good, general utility, and law and order, has thus become the chief issue confronting postcolonial African societies. However, let us note—in opposition to superficial literature on the subject—that the growth of the resources and labor devoted to war, the increase in the number of violent settlings of account, the rise in robbery and the multiple forms of privatizing legal violence indicate more than mere chaos. Behind these processes, it is also important to see current efforts to establish new modalities of legitimate domination and of the gradual reconstruction of formulas of authority founded on other bases.

The hegemony of state administration has thus broken down under the impact of policies of structural adjustment and the slow and patient work carried out by African societies themselves.[125] But neither the anticipated restructuring of the system of the accumulation of productive capital nor the reentry of Africa into regular world markets has taken place. Instead, what is to all appearances a model of economic and social incohesion prevails. The compromises (rules, rights, obligations, counterparts, etc.) that, although costly, guaranteed, up to the beginning of the first oil crisis, the stability of certain postcolonial formulas, have been upset. The effect of disorder and chaos is amplified by the interaction of social protest, the efforts of local tyrannies and their metropolitan supporters to put them down by using force, and the weight of inertia. But what in the short run looks like chaos in fact represents, in the long run, a violent revival of the battles concerning inequality and the control of the means of coercion. This is shown, in addition, by the brutality with which are being renegotiated, at all levels of society, the relationships of loyalty and submission, relations of exchange, reciprocity and coercion, the terms of exclusion and incorporation, in short, the modalities of legitimate subjection.[126] In opposition to approaches that reduce the whole of the historical options in gestation in Africa to a dramatic choice among a "transition" to democracy, a move to the market economy, or a descent into the darkness of war, let us recall the role of chance and reassert the hypothesis that the organizations that result from current developments may well not result from coherent and premeditated plans.

---

[125] See J. F. Bayart, A. Mbembe, and C. Toulabor, *Le politique par le bas. Contribution à une problématique de la démocratie en Afrique noire* (Paris: Karthala, 1992).

[126] See the studies by S. Berry, "Social Institutions and Access to Resources," *Afria* 59 (1984): 41-55; P. E. Peters, "Manoeuvres and Debates in the Interpretation of Land Rights in Botswana," *Africa* 62 (1992): 413-434. In the same issue of *Africa*, see the note by P. Shipton and M. Goheen, "Understanding African Land-Holding: Power, Wealth, and Meaning," 307-325.

## On Private Indirect Government

In the following pages, we must turn away, not only from topical analyses as they are practised by Africanist political science, but also from any kind of Marxist-structural determinism. We must reflect on a series of significant itineraries emerging from current developments, and appearing in outline on the horizon. We shall deepen this analysis by examining a few clues that suggest that another structuring of African societies and a shift in the political and material order that lent them their coherence and relative stability is presently occurring. New institutional arrangements are being tried out. Not all of them are moving toward the consolidation of the state as a general formula of domination and the production of order or toward the institution of a market economy, in accord with canons defined in advance in a doctrinaire manner.[127]

To gauge the significance of the following observations, we should recall the relation between systems of sovereignty and systems of property. The turnabout of African societies is taking place in a context characterized by the gradual dismantling of the state and, in the name of increased efficiency, a refusal to recognize the legitimacy of its intervention in the economic sphere. Some of the consequences of these two processes have been set forth briefly in the first part of this study. Let us add two more that are just as decisive for the future.

First, the policies that have led to the gradual dismantling of public power are based on the idea that as a productive structure, the state has

---

[127] We do not consider these experiments as a deviation or aberration with regard to a so-called norm that is decreed to be unique, all societies being expected to conform to it. They have their own positive character and their own laws. Above all, they are governed by their own reasons and their own protocols. They thus constitute forms of creative interaction with their environment.

failed in Africa and that economic organization governed by the free play of market forces represents the most efficient way of achieving the optimal allocation of resources. The translation of this idea in terms of political economy has led to the sale of public assets, the ending of legal monopolies, concessionary arrangements concerning collective goods and services, changes in customs legislation, and revisions of rates of exchange, among other things—in short, to a partial or total transfer to private individuals of what had been considered public capital. If on a purely economic level, much of our experience suggests that we should minimize the consequences of changes in the ownership of capital and recognize the secondary importance of property in comparison with other criteria (the structure of markets, organizational and strategic choices made by enterprises, the degree of competition, the availability of the factors of labor, relationships between expenses for salaries and productivity, the quality of human capital, etc.), it nonetheless remains that in the African context, these operations fundamentally change the processes of the allocation of wealth (the sharing out of revenues, the regulation of ethno-regional balances) and properly political notions of the public good and the general interest.

Second, in the absence of economic effects per se (a gain in trade based on the exploitation of a comparative advantage), the policies we have just mentioned have opened the way toward a bitter struggle for the concentration and then the privatization of coercion as well as the means that make it possible. The aggravation of these struggles is meaningful only because having such means at one's disposal makes it possible to win an advantage in other struggles currently going on for the appropriation of profits, percentages, and other useful goods formerly concentrated in the hands of the state. In other words, there henceforth exists in Africa a direct connection between the primacy of marketability, the rise of violence, and the establishment of private military, para-military, or jurisdictional organizations.

Several questions follow from these two observations. On the one hand, how does the battle for the concentration of the means of coercion mentioned above operate, and under what conditions will it make it possible to produce what kind of political order on the ruins of the old one? On what other conditions is it likely to eventuate in the defeat of the state itself as a general technology of domination, and what other apparatuses and organizations will it substitute for the latter? On the other hand, since every economy is always underpinned by the use of legal or illegal force, on what conditions can the coercion concentrated in this way be reconverted into the productivity of labor, and on what other conditions is the violence thus set in motion, far from being oriented economically, likely to be transformed into pure disorder and plundering?

A few clues allow us to answer these questions. On the one hand, it is difficult to achieve a concentration of the means of coercion by the use of classical resources, that is, those the state used before the current phase of development. These resources simply no longer exist, or else they are not available in the previous quantities. Ultimately, it is the state itself that no longer exists as a general technology of domination.[128] Nominally, a central power still exists. Its organization chart remains more or less intact, even though the institutions and the bureaucracy that are supposed to embody it have collapsed. Very often, there is no longer any hierarchy or centralized pyramidal organization as such. Orders sent down from the upper levels of the state are seldom carried out, or if they are, never without being twisted and modified in important

---

[128] C. Young and T. Turner, *The Rise and Decline of the Zairian State* (Madison: University of Wisconsin Press, 1985).

ways. Interlocutors constantly change, and at all levels. Official attributions no longer correspond to real and effective powers, and it is not rare that superior authorities are accountable to lower-level authorities. Where real powers exist and are exercised, this is not by virtue of a law or rule, but often on the basis of purely informal, contingent arrangements that can be changed at any time and without warning. Lower levels of authority with respect to the law and the rules have more extensive powers and influence than superior levels. As most of the operations are carried out orally, administrative activity is no longer necessarily recorded in written documents. In practice, no function now presupposes professional training, even if in theory this requirement remains in force. A government official's work no longer really demands total devotion to his duties. The bureaucrat can, in fact, rent out his/her labor or use it to other ends during the time supposed to be devoted, in theory, to the performance of his/her functions. He/she can even sell his/her office and make it a source of emoluments or private revenues which supplement his/her salary, when the latter is still paid. He/she is henceforth in business for himself/herself. In some cases, this labor is no longer even compensated by a salary. A formal budget is set up. But it is adhered to and carried out according to purely contingent and informal criteria. In reality, there is a proliferation, not of autonomous centers of power, but of nuclei and enclaves within the very heart of what until recently took the place of a system. These nuclei and this series of enclaves overlap, are in competition with each other, and sometimes compose networks. They constitute, in any case, the links in a chain that is itself weak and unstable, and in which parallel decisions coexist with centralized decisions. Whence the frequency of short-circuits, the constant changing and twisting of rules, the structurally unpredictably nature of actions, the amalgamation of situations of ossification and inertia with sudden, erratic, and accelerated movements.

93

If such a situation makes it difficult to characterize certain postcolonial African societies as societies without a state, it is nonetheless favorable to the appearance, almost everywhere on the continent, of situations in which there is a quasi-constitutional doubling of power (formal and parallel hierarchies of power, public networks and secret networks...). In order to grasp the import of the various forms taken by the privatization of sovereignty, let us recall once more that the battle for the concentration and then the privatization of the means of coercion took place in a context characterized on the one hand by the worldwide deregulation of markets and movements of money, and on the other by the inability of postcolonial African states to balance their accounts, and even to levy taxes. The supposedly public functions and the tasks of sovereignty are increasingly exercised by private operators for private ends. The soldier and the police officer live off the inhabitants. The official responsible for an administrative service sells the performance of his duties and pockets the proceeds.[129] The question is how such an apparatus of domination is institutionalized and ends up being part of a form of regulation that we have agreed to designate as indirect private government.

We could perhaps make use here of a notion that Max Weber called "unloading," that is, a set of operations whose execution originally lay with the state, but which at a certain moment were taken over by hired hands, henceforth becoming the foundation of the oriental feudal system. According to Weber, the system of unloading had arisen from the degeneration of the monetary economy and the risk run by oriental political systems of falling back into a barter economy.[130] In reality,

---

[129] On this kind of functioning, cf. the notes in A. Mbembe and J. Roitman, "Figures of the Subject in Times of Crisis," *Public Culture* 16 (1995): 341-344.

[130] Weber uses this notion in an effort to contrast East and West and to show that in the East no form of exploitation connected with forced labor developed,

Weber distinguishes among several types of unloading, depending on whether he is discussing Ptolemaic Egypt, India, China, or the Caliphate from the tenth century onward. In some of these models, it happened that levying taxes was put in the hands of private powers or soldiers who paid themselves with the taxes they collected. What was true of levying taxes was also true of the levying of recruits. Thus a set of institutions were gradually set up that, like the institutions of vassalage during the feudal period, enjoyed a comfortable margin of autonomy with regard to both superiors and inferiors. To Weber's mind, the system of unloading as a technique of government and as a procedure of the accumulation of property was not the expression of a cultural trait peculiar to the Orient as such. Moreover, it is the very type of domination that made it possible to administer Rome when the Empire was transformed into a continental state. The difference between unloading in Asia and unloading in the West was based on the fact that in the former, the extortion of payments won out over forms of exploitation connected with forced labor, and this had the effect of increasing the risks of falling back into a barter economy.

The historical sequence presently occurring in Africa is not in precise accord with Weber's model of unloading. On the one hand, while many parts of the continent have fallen back into a barter economy and real demonetarization, the main phenomenon nonetheless remains the practice of barter within a monetary economy, as is shown by the examples of prefinancing of the state's receipts (the early sale of mining resources against budget advances), the massive alienation of mining rights and lands to companies or to private operators who pay annuities. On the other, the general context within which current developments

---

whereas on the other hand the extortion of payments was dominant. Cf. his *General Economic History*, trans. Frank H. Knight (New York: Collier, 1961).

are taking place is one of acute material shortages. The latter have to do first of all with the crisis in subsistence which several countries are experiencing, and which includes various forms of poverty and famine as well as supply problems. To be sure, its intensity varies depending on the region, and the contrasts among wealthy, less wealthy, and impoverished cities and rural areas are striking. But almost everywhere, the population's resources have undergone sometimes drastic decreases, at the very time when pressures of all kinds are growing: taxes and various payments, the dispersion and fragmentation of property, debt, loans against security, the increasing burden of rents, and various kinds of declining status. Finally, the crisis in subsistence has to do with the disruption of the conditions under which Africans determine the value and the price they attribute to all sorts of enterprises and goods, and also the subversion of the equivalences they were accustomed to establish between persons and things, and even life and death.

A central aspect of this crisis in subsistence is the dynamics of the relationships between what could be called "real money" and its opposite, as well as to the extraordinary volatility of prices. Currency devaluations have led nearly everywhere to a drastic drop in the price of non-exchangeable goods. This has been particularly the case for the real remuneration of labor. The inflation of the prices of basic food products has elicited chain reactions. Very frequently, the change in the parity of currencies has had no effect on the competitiveness of economies, while at the same time the bills for imports necessary for production have grown more onerous. The fluctuation of prices and their rise have been accompanied by an unprecedented scarcity of money. As we have already indicated, whole regions have been drawn into a process of eviction from the monetary economy, whereas the ability of the state to extract cash payments in the form of taxes has never been so weak.

As a result of armed conflicts and of the intensive employment of violence required nearly everywhere to restore authoritarianism and to deregulate the economy, the conditions for the establishment of private powers are gradually being realized. In war contexts, this development is manifested by the protection (which may be massive) of unarmed populations that have not been able to find refuge and security elsewhere (delivery of food supplies, firewood, portage, services and charges...). Patrimonies are built up by means of military activities. It also sometimes happens that populations are simply massacred, postcolonial warriors making few efforts to transform themselves into a class of masters controlling people's bodies, whose aim would be to make use of its human patrimony in the framework of exploiting the work force or converting it into a state of dependency. Under these conditions, the goal of war is not economic exploitation. Another economy and other forms of exercising power appear in refugee camps and at places where people are herded together. Revenues are then raised by collecting fees that are in large measure payments for the right to individual protection. Instead of granting fiefs to warriors, most of whom are, increasingly, children, the "warlords" guarantee them the right to take profits and exemptions in kind. This right is exercised by looting stores, houses, and plantations, and by confiscating properties belonging to victims of the war. Because of its episodic and variable character, this right does not allow warriors to subject the unarmed population to forms of forced labor resulting from the control they exercise over their bodies. Everywhere as well, war—but not only war—is accompanied by the rise of a culture of immunity, which explains why protection is assured to private agents proven to be guilty of committing crimes. For example, troops arrogate the right to pillage and rape. Towns and villages are sacked. Natural resources are sold at auction. Death is dealt out publicly, often with a naked blade. Efforts are deliberately made to provoke terror. And no one is prosecuted for anything.

Tax exemptions and judicial immunity are also accorded to those who, occupying dominant positions within what remains of the state apparatus, have been able to convert these positions into opportunities for enriching themselves in the national, regional, and even international circuits of the parallel economy. The same holds true for a certain number of foreign brokers, secret networks, so-called humanitarian organizations that have long been established in these countries or recently set up there. Depending on the circumstances, war and austerity also create the conditions for an extension of domination beyond the limits of the family line. In addition, they promote the formalization of new mechanisms of servitude and dependence. The question is therefore not whether the indices of a system of unloading and the granting of fiefs exist. Rather, the question is under what conditions the private powers currently being established will be able to use coercion to build up patrimonies, to take over the rights of authority and public jurisdictional competencies, to endow themselves with immunities sufficiently deep to allow the crystallization, over the long term, of mechanisms of servitude that are productive and thus able to be the source of a new model of capitalism.

Since we cannot answer these questions at this point, we can only note the appearance, in many countries of the region, of large, armed organizations that are both official and para-official and specialize in the management of coercion—that is, new institutions in charge of administering violence. In fact, armed mechanisms do not perform military functions alone. They also serve as a weapon for establishing properties and restoring arbitrary forms of power. In order to counter the social protest movements that have everywhere accompanied the demand for multi-party politics, most African regimes have unleashed the military (the police, the political police, internal security services, and, if need be, the presidential guard). The latter have been allowed to pay themselves by extorting payments from the general population, first through operations that are supposed to reestablish public order, and then through the daily administration of coercion (road blocks, roundups, forced tax collection, illegal seizures of property, and various kinds of racketeering and preferential treatment). The lack of discipline has helped make it possible to construct bridges between those in power and milieus involved in crime and fraud. In certain countries, the situation has reached a point at which it is no longer excessive to speak of a kind of "tontonmacoutization."[131]

This slide toward "tontonmacoutism" takes several forms. In order to loosen the stranglehold that the campaign of civil and economic disobedience had put on public finances in some countries, seizures and confiscations of property have increased. On the pretext of collecting taxes, the destruction or resale of merchandise also has also become common. In certain cases, sites of production and redistribution have also been occupied militarily. Periodic burning of markets or administrative buildings have taken place, the objective being to punish the merchants, transporters, and other social categories that participated most actively in the protest movements, to destroy evidence of corruption and other compromising documents, and to create shortages, while at the same time monopolizing the sources of essential food supplies. In many cases, troops closed shops at the very moment that the "minor trades" on which lower-class urban groups depended for their subsistence were being attacked. More than those that preceded

---

[131] The expression "tonton-macoute" is borrowed from the Haitian experience. It was originally a Creole term meaning a fantastic, cruel, and frightening figure who carried a straw bag (macoute). Later on, it was used to designate the armed militia set up under the Duvalier regime, one of whose functions was to carry out disreputable assignments for the ruling classes.

it, this new form of coercion has consequently been based on economic issues. But it has also participated in the setting up of new means of political exclusion. In fact, in a context in which the accumulation of overdue payments, advances on mining receipts, and the prefinancing of harvest of cash crops is no longer adequate to refinance the state, the state's clientelization of society no longer operates through putting people on salaries. It is now achieved principally by means of controlling access to the parallel economy. The end of salary as the modality par excellence of clientelizing society and its replacement by "occasional payments" in fact transforms the bases on which rights, transfers, and obligations had previously been converted, and thus the very definitions of postcolonial citizenship. Henceforth, a citizen is a person who can have access to the networks of the parallel economy and to the subsistence incomes that this economy makes possible.

On the other hand, the daily administration of coercion now tends to be decentralized and private: whence the emergence of local cliques that take advantage of this to realize illicit gains and to settle personal accounts. It is no longer only a matter of exploiting bureaucratic positions in the manner of sinecures that bring in extra revenues, trafficking in public power being manifested by a conception of offices as goods that are bought and sold. In certain cases, the situation is such that individuals levy a tax on their subordinates and on the clientele of public service, the army, the police, and the bureaucracy, functioning like a racket sponging on those it administers. As P. Veyne noted with regard to the later Roman Empire, "when things get to this point, we must no longer speak of abuses and corruption: we have to admit that we are confronted by a new and unique historical formation,"[132] a very specific mode of

---

[132] P. Veyne, "Clientèle et corruption au service de l'État: La vénalité des offices dans le Bas-Empire romain," *Annales. Économies. Sociétés. Civilisations.*

governing the conduct of populations, distributing penalties, and handing out benefits.

We are therefore confronted by a mode of deploying force and coercion with its own positive character. Relationships of subjection peculiar to times of shortage and deregulation are being established and institutionalized. These relationships are formed through tolls, extortions, and levies that are in turn connected with a particular conception of command and its circulation through society as a whole. This kind of relationship of subjection is being substituted for the previous one, which consisted in transferring goods and services rendered as mutual counterparts and equivalences. As we have emphasized, the earlier relationship bound people together, not necessarily by means of contracts or agreements, but rather by networks of reciprocal obligations, acts of liberality, praise, and honor that were often manifested by ostentatious expenditures.[133]  On the other hand, the extortions, tolls, and various forms of appropriation of useful goods peculiar to times of austerity appear in a climate of violence in which looting, capture, and pillage become the modalities par excellence of acquiring and consuming wealth.[134]  Liberality as a means of government is thus replaced by debt, forced levies, generalized taxes, and various kinds of payments.

By breaking the bond based on relative reciprocity and transfers of various kinds, and by resorting to unilateral coercion, the agents controlling what remains of postcolonial African states are trying to

---

[133]  J. Warnier, *L'esprit d'entreprise au Cameroun* (Paris: Karthala, 1993); S. Berry, *Fathers Work for their Sons* (Berkeley: University of California Press, 1985), and the same author's *No Condition is Permanent* (Madison: University of Wisconsin Press, 1993).

[134]  J. Guyer, "Wealth in People and Self-Realization in Equatorial Africa," *Man* 1994.

found the state on different bases. In the battles unleashed by this change, those who control the means of coercion have a clear advantage over everyone else. In practice, they can arrogate to themselves the attributes of private seigniory, the public power of the potentate extending to goods as well as persons. Commanding people thus becomes inseparable from making use of their goods. Taxes are transformed into an extensive category that is not dependent on any acquiescence, and their collection is not connected with any precise idea of public utility or common advantage. Moreover, the levying of taxes is no longer one of the aspects of the state monopoly of coercion, but rather of the state's loss of this monopoly and its dispersion within the society. Henceforth, there is no difference between taxes and exactions.

Finally, the privatization of public violence and its use in the service of the goal of private enrichment has as its corollary the accelerated development of a shadow economy over which elements of the police, the army, and the customs and tax services seek to tighten their control (trafficking in drugs, counterfeit money, arms, and toxic wastes, customs fraud, etc.). Because of austerity policies, large segments of society depend on the shadow economy for their daily subsistence, beyond any salaried work or direct patronage on the part of those in power, and if this kind of control is achieved, they could end up being driven out of this sector. What is therefore at stake is the possibility of new modalities of subjecting and controlling people. The importance of the international support afforded to this process of solidifying authoritarianism, particularly in francophone countries, has not been sufficiently emphasized. The extraordinary influence exercised by "networks" and private lobbies, the significance of the military element, and the perversion of bureaucratic logics have made possible the consolidation in these countries of guaranteed incomes that are drawn, not only by the indigenous potentates, but also by a whole range of brokers, businessmen, mercenaries, and operators with connections in the intelligence milieu, the army, and sometimes the underworld. The wheeling and dealing that already characterized Gaullist networks was amplified and intensified under cover of managing privatizations, debts, gifts, loans, advances and subsidies, tax deductions and various kinds of credits. Today, corruption and venality are present in almost all sectors, even the diplomatic services.

With the help of privatization and programs of structural adjustment, a concessionary economy—composed of lucrative monopolies, secret contracts, private arrangements, and preferential treatments in the areas of tobacco, transportation, port operations, agro-industry, large equipment supply, petroleum, uranium, lithium, manganese, weapons purchases, the training and supervision of armies and tribal militias, and the recruitment of mercenaries—is currently being set up. A process, not of marginalization, as is claimed, but rather of the conjunction and interlacing of the international networks of foreign traffickers, brokers, and financiers with local businessmen and "technocrats" is thus taking place, and driving underground whole areas of Africa's international economic relations.

Symptomatic in this regard is what looks very much like an exhaustion of the model of the territorial state, characterized by institutional differentiation, the centrality and verticality of the political relationship, spatial demarcation, a monopoly on the exercise of legitimate violence, and authorized tax levies.[135] The dogma of the "intangibility of boundaries inherited from colonialism" in fact receives little respect—not, of course, in the sense that we are witnessing uncontrollable rises

---

[135] Cf. M. Weber, *Economy and Society* (New York: Bedminster Press, 1968); C. Tilly, *The Formation of National States in Western Europe* (Princeton: Princeton University Press, 1975).

of separatist fever leading to an irreversible destruction of the territorial framework of postcolonial states like that that has taken place in Yugoslavia (with the exception of Ethiopia), but rather in the sense that the pressures of identity politics, the dynamics of autonomy and differentiation, the various forms of ethno-regionalism, migratory pressures, the inflation of the religious, and the accelerated decline of African societies into the so-called parallel economy are profoundly changing the spatial and social organization of the continent, the distribution of its populations, and the real functioning of markets, thereby shifting the material foundations of power.

In all the countries where the sociopolitical configurations were already so distinct before the European occupation, regional differentiations have been accentuated, firstly as a result of colonial policies of "developing" the lands conquered in the nineteenth century, and secondly as a result of the forms taken by political control since the end of direct colonization. In many cases, the gap between the formal stability of the borders and their economically and culturally changing character steadily increased. Structures of conflict appeared almost everywhere where ethnic groups claiming to enjoy the right to citizenship by virtue of having been born in the country considered themselves to be looked down upon by a majority of "allogenes." The construction of the feeling of belonging and the reinvention of identities was increasingly carried out through disputes about heritages and through manipulating the ideology based on being autochthonous and having autochthonous ancestors. Whole zones, whether or not they are occupied by armed gangs, are without any civil authority.

Thanks to these dynamics of territorial regrouping and spatial dislocation, the real map of the continent is itself being reshaped around regional and international axes of exchange and trafficking which in large measure simultaneously intersect and transcend the historical spheres of expansion and commercial dynamism of the nineteenth century.[136] The same is true of the old caravan trails on the perimeter of the Sahel, Atlantic routes, the ivory and precious stones operations linking Senegambia with Katanga[137] and later Katanga with southern Africa, trafficking around the Red Sea and the Indian Ocean, trade around the Nilotic-speaking areas, and whole zones where a multiplicity of currencies coexisted and were exchanged outside official structures, sometimes with the encouragement of the formal bureaucracies, and increasingly under the control of what remains of the tax authorities, the judicial system, and especially the military.

As for the rest, the social and economic importance assumed by borders is currently acquiring political meanings. Borders no longer merely separate one country from another, but tend to become internal to the countries themselves (this is the case for certain regions of the Congo, Angola, Uganda, the Sudan, and countries around the Sahara).[138] The autonomization of whole regions, the reversion to the state of geographical pockets that have been more or less emptied of their inhabitants and the reversion of gaps and intermediary spaces within a single state, and the concentration of populations around river basins

---

[136] J. R. Gray and D. Birmingham, *Pre-Colonial African Trade: Essays on Trade in Central and Eastern Africa Before 1900* (London, 1970); C. Meillassoux, *The Development of Indigenous Trade and Markets in West Africa* (London, 1971); P. Lovejoy and S. Baier, "The Desert-Side Economy of the Central Sudan," *International Journal of African Historical Studies* 7 (1975): 551-581; A. J. H. Latham, "Currency, Credit and Capitalism on the Cross River in the Pre-Colonial Era," *Journal of African History* 12 (1971): 249-260.

[137] S. Bredeloup, "L'aventure des diamantaires sénégalais," *Politique africaine* 56 (1994): 77-93.

[138] J. MacGaffey, ed., *The Real Economy of Zaire* (London: James Currey, 1992).

and regional ecological zones thus constitute characteristic traits of an increasing number of countries. Similarly, whole provinces of certain countries are being turned into satellites of their neighbors. In some places, these processes are accompanied by an unprecedented resurgence of territorial identities, an extraordinary emphasis on family and clan lineages and on birthplaces, and a revival of the dynamism of the ethnic imagination. In most of the great urban centers confronted by land problems, distinctions between outsiders (those who have come from somewhere else, who have immigrated) and autochthonous residents (those who were born on the land itself and have always lived in the same place) have become common.[139] This proliferation of internal boundaries—whether imaginary or symbolic, and whether they are connected primarily with economic struggles or with battles for power—and the exacerbation of local affiliations, which is its corollary gave rise to practices of exclusion, closure based on identity, and persecution that can easily lead, as we have already seen, to genuine pogroms and even to genocides.[140]

Alongside these dynamics of reterritorialization, a specific form of violence is developing: war. Let us note in this respect that in the context of the economic contraction and depression mentioned earlier, most of the wars, although they have disastrous consequences in the short and the long term, are nonetheless small wars. Even when they involve the armed forces of one or several countries, they are in general

---

[139] Cf. certain examples in S. Jaglin and A. Dubresson, eds., *Pouvoirs et cités d'Afrique noire* (Paris: Karthala, 1993).

[140] See, for example, R. LeMarchand, *Burundi: Ethnocide as Discourse and Practice* (Cambridge: Cambridge University Press, 1994); F. M. Deng, *War of Visions: Conflict of Identities in the Sudan* (Washington DC: The Brookings Institution, 1995).

wars carried out by gangs, and very often wars of plundering, opposing one group of predators to another. Like certain medieval wars, they involve a small number of troops and relatively primitive weapons. While their tactics are fairly rudimentary, they nonetheless lead to catastrophes. The military pressure sometimes aims, in fact, at the pure and simple destruction of the civilian population's means of subsistence (food reserves, livestock, agricultural implements). Pillage and extortion are not rare. In a certain number of cases, these wars have allowed gang leaders to exercise more or less continual control over more or less extensive parts of territories. This kind of control gives them access not only to the populations on these territories, but also to their resources and to the goods that are produced there. The financing of the wars being carried on is very complex. It does not suffice, in fact, to ransom, to live off the country or to pillage it.

In addition to the financial support provided by those in diaspora and the levying of workers assigned to obligatory or forced labor for porterage or troop supply, we must also mention the recourse to borrowing, the appeal to private financiers, the granting of concessions (in forestry and mining) and the emergence of special kinds of taxes. To levy men, and especially to equip them, funds are obtained from companies working a vein located in the part of the territory controlled by a faction. These companies continue to develop the resource or mineral, which they later export to the world market. In return, they transfer large sums of money to those who control this part of the territory, whether by bills of exchange or by other means (the disbursement of cash, for instance, or allocations in kind). This war taxation also includes various financial expedients, such as fines, licenses, and extortions, the confiscation of fixed assets, and forcing conquered or occupied territories to make payments.

It has also happened that after a given length of time, a fragmentation of this control takes place, dissensions having developed within the group. Everywhere where it occurs, military activity leads to a rearrangement of the ways in which lands, goods, and populations are administered, as well as to a transformation of the forms in which resources are levied and distributed and the frameworks within which disputes are resolved. Where war happens, it does not necessarily lead, as it does in Europe, to the development of the state apparatus or to the latter's monopolization of the use of force within its boundaries. Under present conditions, the connection between war and the emergence of an uncontested central power is not in any way mechanical in nature. However, it is true that military activity is one of the means by which new formulas of domination are being shaped on the continent. In certain cases, a reconfigured state prevails and is transformed, if necessary, into the principal technology of this domination. This is not the case in many other circumstances. Here, as in other domains, we must also take into account the interlacing of local and international interests. Nonetheless, war situations require the renegotiation of the relationships between individual and community, the bases on which authority is exercised, the relationship to time, profit, and the invisible.[141]

## The Public Good and Fiscal Regulation

The distinction between a state of war and a state of peace is itself increasingly factitious. Activities of extortion and, more generally, the power to make use of things and people are not peculiar to contexts in

---

[141] Cf. T. Allen, "Understanding Alice: Uganda's Holy Spirit Movement in Context," *Africa* 61 (1991): 370-399. See also K. Wilson, "Cults of Violence and Counterviolence in Mozambique," *Journal of Southern African Studies* 18 (1992): 527-582.

which war erupts. Often, they have only a distant connection with fiscal activity proper, since they are confined to the sphere of simple subsistence. Violence that is real and economically oriented, whether it takes the form of military activity or plundering, is in fact directly related to the notion of taxation, and consequently to the problematics of the construction or destruction of the state. As a result, throughout its history, taxation has been the determining economic foundation of the state, just as a monopoly on legitimate violence has been one of the keys to the process of state-building. It was through taxation that the conversion of force and arbitrariness into authority, of coercion into exchange, took place. In the West, for example, taxation has always been more than a simple price to be paid, even for public services. To be sure, by paying taxes, the individual subject contributes, qua individual, to the public spending for which everyone pays, although he may of course derive from it certain private satisfactions. But it is never the individual as such who determines how much of his income to reserve for the state. In fact, the financial and economic calculations required by taxation always involve that other power that is the state, and through the state, the different social groups that are battling, opposing, and compromising with each other. Finally, the collective coercion inherent in the fiscal relationship never wholly eliminates the possibility of a relationship of exchange between taxpayers and the state. It is this relationship of exchange—through which the fiscal subject "purchases" claims on the state—that distinguishes political democracies from systems based on coercion and arbitrary power, since in the latter case what is called the common good or public utility is never supposed to be subject to genuine public debate.

Let us return now to the dimension of violence as such, and note that the beginning of taxation is always related to coercion. In African history, the locus where its relationship with violence is most clearly manifested was and is war. This relationship revealed itself in the form of the booty that the winners seized at the end of a war. This booty allowed them to pay their soldiers and to feed them, war itself sometimes being turned into an opportunity for self-enrichment. In most cases, however, and despite all sorts of protocols, the taking of booty occurred in a disorderly manner, often through mere pillaging, and lasted only as long as the raiding party was in the area. Over the long term, its productivity was unpredictable, because pillaging exhausted capital without necessarily leading to an increase in goods. Basically, the raids were destructive in character. The raided population was not left in possession of its goods. Its products, what it most prized, were lost. Its labor was wasted. And where people had been able to survive, only terror and fear remained. The material devastation could be extensive, and the transfer of wealth, the acquisition of profits, and the prospects of ransom gained through pillaging often resulted in the disorganization of commerce and credit. On the other hand, this kind of relationship created a bond for only a short time, that of the conquest itself. The latter might or might not be followed by an occupation or the creation of a protectorate that had to pay tribute. It was therefore a purely summary act, almost without counterpart.

We can say that then as now, the question of taxation arises as a political question as soon as efforts are made to control disorder, to lay down the law, to reign in private violence, and to produce order. Historically, the problem of controlling private violence was resolved by levying a tribute or by requisitioning goods or forced labor. In these three cases, the subjected groups often retained the freedom to earn a living, even though, being compelled to work without compensation, they were often taken away from their daily occupations. But part of their resources, their time, their labor, and what they produced was handed over to their masters, whether in kind or, later on, in monetary form. What characterized this sort of commerce was the strong element of arbitrariness. The political significance of taxation at the dawn of modern times emerged as soon as people became concerned with converting this arbitrariness into a reciprocal obligation, binding on both sovereign and subject, a close relation having thereby been established between the institution of taxation, on the one hand, and the process of granting people political enfranchisement and citizenship on the other.

In Western countries, as we know, this process went on over a long period and was connected with profound transformations of social structures, commerce, the means of waging war, legal technologies, ways of conceiving of the public good and general utility, and the relationships among the state, society, and the market. Let us examine, for example, the case of France. Originally, the royal tax was called an aide, fouage, or a subside. It was only later on that it was called the taille.[142] The fouage was distinguished from the aide in that it was a charge paid by each household, whereas a subside was support paid to an individual or a group as a subsidy or in payment for services rendered. That was how custom operated, moreover. In the logic of the relationships between lords and vassals, the king was obliged to derive his revenue from his own domain, just like other lords of his time. But the rules of feudalism also provided that if need be, and especially in order to supplement revenues from its own domain, the monarchy could call for temporary

---

[142] Literally, an *aide* is help given a person or a entity that is in need. The payer acts on its behalf, joining his efforts to those of the person or entity in question. An *aide* is by nature temporary. When it is continually levied it becomes extraordinary. An *aide* cannot be extorted. The receiver is dependent upon the giver.

aides within a framework set by custom. The taille was a kind of payment levied by lords within the framework of feudalism. Only after royal authority had supplanted customary authorities, broken their resistance, and moved beyond the authorization, which it was supposed to receive from the Estates General, did it begin to make use of the taille. All civilians—that is, non-combatants—were required to make this payment.

The taille was based on three ideas. On the one hand, by paying it civilians bought exemption from conscription, and this allowed them to avoid taking part directly in the incessant wars of the period, while at the same time guaranteeing them the possession of the rest of their possessions that were thus to be protected. On the other hand, the taille was levied only on an exceptional and temporary basis, at least originally. As an extraordinary "tax" and an institution peculiar to wartime, there was no reason, in theory at least, for it to survive, once the ground for levying it had ceased to exist. Finally, it was not one of the monarch's rights. Not being a regular duty owed the sovereign by his subjects, it could be levied only with the taxpayers' assent.[143] It is therefore clear that at the outset, one of the functions of taxation was to acquire the means to wage war (men, supplies, money, weapons). Taxation played a very important role in very formation of Western states to the extent that its institution was inseparable from setting up a vast military and tax-collecting apparatus. The establishment of such a centralized apparatus was part of a long process that was concurrent with the transition from the right to wage war privately (which feudal lords claimed and exercised until the end of the Middle Ages) to the idea of the monarch's prerogative to wage war as a sovereign and as responsible for maintaining public order. In this measure, taxation was instrumental in the

---

[143] On these observations and the preceding ones, see G. Ardant, *Histoire de l'impôt*; E. Esmonin, *La Taille en Normandie au temps de Colbert, 1661-1683* (Geneva: Mégariotis Reprints, 1978), 2-10.

emergence and development of two mutually connected concepts, those of public authority and the common good.

These two concepts were developed and confirmed in opposition to customary usage, which consisted in resorting to private violence to avenge oneself. Slowly, the notion of public authority exercised in the common interest won out over the right to private violence.[144] A monopoly on violence and a monopoly on taxation, then, the one justifying the other.[145] But in both Western countries and African history, there has never been taxation without a certain organization of coercion, that is, a way of "mistreating one's subjects," of administering them, of guaranteeing the exploitation and domination of people. Organizing coercion in the most efficient possible way always presupposed that stable control had been established over the population of a given territory. This kind of control was meaningful only if it authorized access to part of the resources, goods, and services produced in this territory.

Thus we are confronted by two contradictory tendencies. On the one hand, since the Roman era one principle has been generally acknowledged and appealed to by legislators whenever the need arose: the right to tax is one of the attributes of sovereign authority (the idea of the authority to tax). On the other hand, consent to be taxed gradually

---

[144] Cf. R. W. Kaeuper, *Guerre, justice et ordre public. La France et l'Angleterre à la fin du Moyen Âge*, trans. N. Genet and J. P. Genet (Paris: Aubier, 1994): 220-226.

[145] N. Elias: "...la force armée concentrée entre les mains du pouvoir central garantit la collecte des contributions, et la concentration des denrées fiscales dans les caisses de l'administration central consolide la monopolisation de la contrainte physique, de la force militaire, ces deux moyens de puissance se renforçant réciproquement." In *La dynamique de l'occident* (Paris: Calman Levy, 1975), 170. See also L. Von Stein, "On Taxation," in Musgrave and Peacock, *Classics in the Theory of Public Finance* (New York: Macmillan, 1967), 28-36.

became a principle of public law: the sovereign did not have the right to levy taxes at will outside his own domain. And to obtain the consent of lords and provincial states, he had to show that he had exceptional needs. Thus there was a tension between the free and voluntary character of taxation and its coercive dimension. These are two theories of levies that oppose each other until they are reconciled in democratic regimes. The tradition that was extended to the colonies in the nineteenth century was, however, the one in which the state, in the figure of the king, is the master of the life, the honor, and the goods of his subjects. According to this tradition, the subjects possess their goods only as usufruct. In reality, property belongs to the king and to the state by right of sovereignty. The king and the state merely allow subjects the use of these goods. In certain cases, moreover, the sovereign may make use of individuals' goods against their will. As a result, in requiring the payment of taxes, the state and the king are only reclaiming part of what is their own. Further, according to this tradition, taxation is justified, on the one hand, by the need to safeguard public prosperity and the common good; on the other, it is explained by the concern to ensure obedience on the part of the sovereign's subjects. It is in this sense that it is a quintessential mark of subjection. Thanks to taxation, subjects never forget their condition, since in the words of Richelieu, "if they were freed from the payment of tribute, they would think themselves freed from obedience as well." Like mules, they have to be accustomed to bear their burden.[146]

---

[146] On these debates, cf. Richelieu, *Testament politique*, vol. 1, p. 225; Bossuet, *Politique tirée de l'Écriture sainte*, vol. 6, ii, part. 3; Lebret, *De la souveraineté du roy*, bk. 3, chap. 7; Lacour-Gayet, *L'Éducation politique de Louis XIV*, bk. 2, chap. 7; Bodin, *De la république*, bk. 1, chap. 8; La Mothe le Vayer, *La politique du prince* (Paris, 1655).

## Conclusion

Let us return to the case of Africa, and emphasize that in the contexts described above, a new form of the organization of power, based on the control of the principal means of coercion (armed force, means of intimidation, imprisonment, expropriation, killings) is emerging in the framework of territories that no longer constitute states in the full sense. The borders of these territories are more or less delimited, though they may change in accord with the vagaries of military action. The exercise of the right to levy, the monopolization of supplies, tributes, tolls of all kinds, rents, taxes, tithes and exactions makes it possible to maintain bands of soldiers and something like a civil apparatus and coercion, while at the same time participating in international networks (both formal and informal) of the circulation of money and wealth (ivory, diamonds, wood, minerals) among states. That is the case, for example, in all the countries where the process of privatization has been combined with war, and has been based on a unprecedented interlacing of the interests of brokers, financiers, and international businessmen with those of local plutocrats.[147]

Whatever the point of view, it is therefore the setting up of another political economy and the invention of different systems of coercion and other strategies of exploitation that we currently find in Africa. For the moment, the question is whether these processes will or will not eventuate in the emergence of a system of capitalized coercion sufficiently coherent to impose changes on the organization of production and the class structure of African societies. Or whether the subjection of Africans that they require, the exclusion and the inequalities to which

---

[147] For details, see W. Reno's study, *Corruption and State Politics in Sierra Leone* (Cambridge: Cambridge University Press, 1995).

they lead, will succeed in legitimating themselves and their corollary violence socialized to the point of becoming once again a public good. One may also wonder to what extent the violence (pillaging, riots, extortion) and inequality that are inherent in these processes may be precipitating the destruction of the "civility" acknowledged to be an eminent trait of all citizenship. The fiscal crisis, shortages, and the population movements that go along with these reconstructions lead one to think that for the moment it is a matter of a simple battle between predators. But there is no reason to conclude that, in the long term, prosperity and democracy cannot arise out of crime. In the meantime, outside the sphere of the state, new forms of belonging and social incorporation (the constitution of various "leagues," "corporate bodies," and "coalitions") are in gestation. There is in fact no doubt that most of the religious and therapeutic movements that are currently proliferating in Africa constitute (though they are not reducible to) sites of visibility— ambiguous, to be sure—where new normative systems and new common languages are being negotiated, and new authorities being constituted. But here again, nothing allows us to conclude that the increase of these "separate spheres" and their assertion in the public space reflects anything other than a heteronomous, fragmented conception of the "political community."

The basic question, that of the emergence of a legal subject, thus remains wholly unresolved. The history of other regions of the world shows that taxation is what has served to define, beyond interpersonal allegiances, the connection between the governed and the government. The state no doubt had the means to "obligate" legal subjects. But at least in theory, it could obligate them only by obligating itself. It had the right to levy taxes only insofar as its subjects, represented in assemblies, exercised their rights with regard to the levies and to the forms in which the money raised by them would be used or spent. It

116

was through this process that the state could define itself as a common good and no longer solely as a relationship of domination. It was also through this process that the state converted its power to obligate by obligating itself into the power to dictate the law. Finally, it was through this process that the subject gained a status in the political order, to the extent that by paying taxes and exercising a right over their use, he objectified legally his political role as a citizen. The subject objectified this role by entering into a set of rights and obligations with the state, which thereby endowed itself with public credibility precisely because it used its sovereign power in a way that respected the law. On the path of political modernity, that may be the only way to move forward.

www.ingramcontent.com/pod-product-compliance
Lightning Source LLC
Chambersburg PA
CBHW071136280326
41935CB00010B/1247